I0529981

The Double Life of a High-Functioning Alcoholic

Addiction, Lies, and the Courage to Quit Drinking Alcohol

Howard Kane

Hidden Alpha Capital LLC

Copyright © 2025 by Howard Kane

All rights reserved.

No part of this publication may be reproduced, distributed, or transmitted in any form
or by any means, including photocopying, recording, or other electronic or mechanical
methods, without the prior written permission of the publisher, except as permitted by
U.S. copyright law. For permission requests, contact https://selfcarejourneybooks.com
/contact/.

The story, all names, characters, and incidents portrayed in this production are fictitious.
No identification with actual persons (living or deceased), places, buildings, and prod-
ucts is intended or should be inferred.

1st edition in 2025

About Author

H OWARD KANE KNOWS WHAT it feels like to look successful while quietly struggling with habits that feel impossible to break. As an executive at a Fortune 500 company, Howard
spent years hiding his worries behind late nights and busy work-
days. He understands the silent doubts of high achievers who tell
themselves that a few drinks every night is normal.

When Howard finally faced the truth about his drinking, his life
began to change. He rebuilt his world through self-care, honest
reflection, and practical habits that anyone can use. His first mem-
oir-style novel, *The Double Life of a High-Functioning Alcoholic*, is
inspired by this journey. This book is more than just a story about
addiction. It is a lifeline for anyone who wonders if their drinking
might be a bigger problem than they think.

With honest writing and real experience, Howard offers hope
and a path to lasting change. If you have ever questioned your
relationship with alcohol, this book was written for you. Discover
how one honest choice can lead to a better life. Start your new

chapter with The Double Life of a High-Functioning Alcoholic today.

Contents

Chapter One

The Invisible Line

I WASN'T THE KIND of guy who was supposed to have a drinking problem.

That thought pulsed through my head as I stared into the hotel bathroom mirror, clutching the sink like it might steady the panic in my chest. The place was high-end. Sleek marble, soft lighting, one of those fancy hotels in Manhattan where the soap smells like eucalyptus. We were there for my company's big data science summit. I was supposed to be the calm, collected director, the guy running a global team, presenting on machine learning pipelines, shaking hands with VPs.

Instead, I was hiding.

My hands trembled just enough to betray me. Not so anyone would notice. I'd become too good at that. I kept them under the table during meetings, wrapped around a mug of black coffee like it was armor, or buried deep in my blazer pockets while I gave polished presentations.

1

"Everything okay in there, Dave?" my VP called through the door.

I flinched.

"Yep! All good. Be right out," I said, way too casually.

I turned on the tap and let the cold water run over my wrists. That trick had worked before. I took a few deep breaths, stared at myself in the mirror, and straightened my tie. When I walked back out into the ballroom, I looked like I had it all together.

No one could tell I'd blacked out the night before. Again.

No one knew I'd woken up at 3 a.m. with my heart pounding, scrolling through texts, trying to piece together what I'd said to my team at the happy hour. Or whether I'd embarrassed myself. Again.

I was forty-four. Married, with a son who thought I hung the moon. From the outside, things looked great. I had a career most people would kill for, leading a team of twenty data scientists spread across three continents. I could talk about neural nets and predictive models like I was reciting the alphabet.

And I could also outdrink a room full of consultants, then be up at six the next morning for a client call like nothing happened.

From the outside, I was the furthest thing from an "alcoholic." I didn't drink in the mornings. Never touched vodka in the garage. I could go a week (sometimes two) without a drop. I just liked to "unwind." You know, the way a lot of high-performing, over-caffeinated professionals do. The problem was, "unwind" had quietly morphed into "unravel."

The cracks were small at first. A foggy memory here. A missed bedtime story there. A few too many on a Thursday night that turned into an argument with my wife over nothing.

But that day in the hotel bathroom, something shifted. I couldn't ignore the signs anymore. My body was jittery. My mind was racing. And underneath the mask of composure, I felt like a guy dangling from a cliff edge, pretending he was just out for a scenic hike.

I once read that the most dangerous part of drinking isn't going from sober to drunk. It's crossing that invisible line between drinking in control and drinking that quietly controls you. The catch is, you don't notice when you've crossed it. You just wake up one day and realize the line's behind you.

This isn't a story about a dramatic rock bottom. I didn't crash my car. I didn't lose my job or get arrested. My life, from the outside, still looked perfectly intact. But inside, I was slowly unraveling.

And that's the thing no one tells you. Alcohol doesn't have to wreck your life overnight to be a problem. Sometimes, it erodes you in tiny, invisible ways. It chips away at your clarity, your confidence, your peace of mind. It steals the little moments: the bedtime stories, the weekend mornings, the honest conversations. And you don't even realize how much you've lost until you try to stop.

This memoir isn't about rock bottom. It's about the gray area where everything still looks okay, but nothing feels right. It's about the long, messy decision to quit drinking when everyone around you says, "But you don't have a problem." It's about making that decision, anyway.

It's also about what happens next. Because quitting isn't some magical fix. It's not an overnight glow-up. It's a quiet revolution. One day at a time, one awkward social event at a time, one lonely Friday night at a time. You trade numbness for clarity, which sounds great until you remember how much easier life was to ignore when you were a little buzzed.

But here's the thing. Clarity, even when it hurts, is worth it.

My story doesn't begin with disaster. It begins with a mirror, a pair of shaking hands, and a man realizing that something has to change. It begins in that foggy, familiar space between "I'm fine" and "I'm not." And maybe that's where your story begins too.

If you've ever looked at your life and thought, This looks great on paper, so why do I feel like I'm falling apart? This is for you.

If you've ever asked yourself, Do I really need to stop? Even as some small, honest part of you whispers, Maybe you do. Then yeah, this is definitely for you.

It's for all of us who weren't "supposed" to have a problem, but found ourselves face-to-face with one, anyway.

Chapter Two

The First Taste

S ITTING ON THE COLD bathroom floor of that Manhattan hotel, hands still shaking, I kept circling back to one question: How did I end up here? When did drinking for fun turn into drinking just to function? There was no dramatic moment that marked the change. The story really started over twenty years earlier with a simple invitation and a lie I told myself about being able to handle anything that came my way.

Senior year of high school, 1998. I was seventeen and every little thing seemed to carry life-or-death importance. Katie Morrison stood at her locker, talking to Jake Stevens about the weekend. Jake was everything I wanted to be: confident, relaxed, the kind of guy who could fit in anywhere.

I hung around, pretending to search my backpack while I listened in.

"My parents are going to my aunt's wedding this weekend," Katie said. "You guys should come over Saturday night."

My heart was pounding. Katie was throwing a party. This was the same Katie I had a crush on since tenth grade, but never had the guts to ask out.

I told myself this was my chance. Every movie I watched said all I needed was the courage to speak up. If I was honest, I could win her over.

My legs felt heavy as I forced myself to walk over. My mouth was dry, but in my head I could hear my father saying, "Dave, you're just as smart as those kids."

I took a shaky breath and joined the conversation.

"Hey, Katie," I said, voice a little thin. "Um, your party sounds fun. Is it okay if I come?"

She turned, smiling in that way she always did. "Of course, Dave. You should come."

I almost asked her to say it again, just to make sure I heard right. Katie Morrison had just invited me to her party.

The rest of that week, I was caught somewhere between excitement and panic. My best friend, Marcus Chen, tried to bring me down to earth.

"You know there's going to be drinking, right?" he asked at lunch.

"So?" I replied, already searching the internet for 'how to be cool at parties.'

"You've never even had a drink before."

He was right. My family had a long history of alcohol problems, and my parents always warned me to be careful. They talked about addiction like it was a shadow that could fall over anyone if you were not paying attention.

"It's not about the drinking," I told Marcus. "It's about finally feeling like I belong."

By Saturday night, I had convinced myself this party would change everything. Maybe after this, I would stop being invisible.

Katie's house was in one of those perfect suburban neighborhoods where every yard looked manicured and every porch light was on. I parked three blocks away, partly because the street was full, but mostly because I didn't want anyone to see our old, dented Honda Civic.

As I walked up to the door, I could hear music and laughter spilling out onto the lawn. I rang the bell and rehearsed something clever to say.

Katie answered, casually in jeans and a sweater. "Dave! You made it!"

I followed her inside. The living room was filled with twenty or so kids from our class. This wasn't the wild party from the movies. It felt more grown-up, which somehow made me even more aware of my khakis and button-down shirt.

I found my way to the snack table and loaded up on chips, pretending I knew what I was doing. I watched the room and tried to work up the nerve to talk to anyone. Jake was at the center of it all, making everyone laugh.

I was thinking about making up an excuse to leave when Jake looked over and spotted me.

"Hey, brain boy! Glad you made it," he called out, waving me over.

To my surprise, he seemed genuinely happy I was there. He even moved over on the couch to make space for me.

"Davies, you look like you're about to have a panic attack," he teased, grinning.

He was not wrong. My shoulders were tense and my smile felt forced. I probably looked like I was about to bolt for the door.

That was the moment Jake reached into a cooler and pulled out a beer.

The can in Jake's hand was ice-cold, little drops of condensation forming on the outside. He held it out to me, casual as ever, like passing a drink was just the most natural thing to do.

"This will help you loosen up, man."

I stared at the beer as if it might explode. In seventeen years, nobody my age had ever offered me alcohol.

"I don't really drink," I said, which was the understatement of my life.

Jake grinned and shrugged off my hesitation. "That's even better. Tonight is your big initiation. Welcome to the real world, Davies."

The real world. Sometimes it felt like my parents' warnings about alcohol had just kept me on the outside of everything. Maybe there was something here I was supposed to learn about being normal.

I looked around. Everyone had a drink. Beer cans, red cups. Even Marcus, who had warned me about this, stood by the fireplace with a beer in his hand, deep in conversation.

Jake leaned in a little closer. "You're smart, Davies, but you overthink everything. Sometimes you have to just trust yourself."

That sounded like advice for a science test, but maybe it applied here too.

I took the beer from him. It felt heavy and colder than I expected, almost numbing my hand. I pulled the tab, and the sharp hiss made a few people glance over. Suddenly, I felt very exposed.

The smell was nothing like I expected. Sharp and yeasty, not at all like anything I thought grown-up drinks should smell like. I hesitated, then raised the can and took my first sip.

The taste was terrible. Bitter, harsh, nothing pleasant about it. I wanted to set the can down and forget the whole thing, but I could feel eyes on me. Katie had wandered over to our group and seemed curious to see what I would do.

I swallowed and tried not to let my face show how bad it was.

"Not bad, right?" Jake said.

I nodded, not trusting myself to speak. Still, I noticed something changing almost right away. A warm feeling started in my chest, a little bubble of relaxation that felt new and strangely welcome.

Katie took a seat across from us. "How do you feel?"

"Good," I answered, surprised by how easy my voice sounded. "Different, but good."

She smiled. "Different how?"

I took another sip, focusing on the feeling more than the taste this time. The warmth kept spreading, and the room seemed to soften around the edges. Conversations were easier to follow. My anxiety felt lighter.

"It's like everything isn't so intense," I said.

Jake clinked his can against mine. "Welcome to the club, Davies."

The second sip was easier. After half the can, I noticed the people around me started to make more sense. I was no longer over-analyzing every word, every look. I was just there, listening.

Jake launched into a story about last weekend's football game. Normally, I would have been in my head, worrying about how to respond. This time, I just listened and when he mentioned calling an audible, I found myself asking, "What's that?"

"It means changing the play at the last minute," Jake said. "Sometimes you have to go with your gut instead of the plan."

That sounded familiar. I shared how my best SAT scores came from trusting my first instinct.

Katie leaned in, interested. "What did you get?"

"Fifteen eighty," I answered, and then worried I sounded full of myself.

Jake let out a low whistle. "That's incredible, Davies."

"Amazing," Katie said, and the warmth inside me grew. For a moment, I was just happy. No calculations, no rehearsing what to say next.

I kept talking, words coming easily now. "The stress was the worst part. I kept thinking about how much was riding on that test."

Sarah Martinez, who I barely knew, joined in. "I hate that pressure. Why should four hours on a Saturday decide your entire future?"

I agreed. "The sections I stressed over most were my lowest scores. Anxiety just makes you dumber."

Everyone nodded. I took another sip, barely noticing the taste. Everything felt easier.

For the first time, I felt like I finally fit in. For a little while, I felt normal.

Jake handed me a second beer without saying a word. This time, I did not hesitate. The taste was already less harsh, almost neutral now. What mattered more was how my mind felt. I was not slower, just less cluttered. Everything seemed easier.

HOWARD KANE

"So what's MIT going to be like?" Sarah asked as she sat down next to me on the couch.

Sarah Martinez was talking to me by choice. Three hours ago, I would have been too anxious to get a sentence out.

"Hopefully like this," I said, motioning around the room, "but with a lot more calculus."

Everyone laughed, and it was genuine laughter, not just polite agreement.

"You're way funnier than I thought," Katie said, and I felt a different kind of warmth, one that had nothing to do with alcohol.

Way funnier than she thought. That meant she had thought about me before. I had never considered that.

I was getting the hang of this, whatever this was. Making conversation, being part of things, just showing up as myself. And the beer seemed to be the key. Not drinking to get drunk, but finding just the right amount, so my usual anxiety dropped away and my personality could actually come through.

"The real problem with high school," I said, ideas coming out fast and easy, "is that everyone is pretending to be someone they're not. We're all acting out these roles we think we're supposed to play."

Katie nodded like she understood. "Yes. Like, I'm supposed to be the perfect student government president, but half the time I have no clue what I'm doing."

"You seem pretty natural at it," I said.

12

"That's just because I'm getting better at faking confidence," she admitted. "Inside, I'm terrified I'm about to mess everything up."

I stared at her. Katie, nervous about screwing up? The same girl who could give speeches to the entire school?

"Everyone's got their own stuff going on," Jake said. "The trick is not letting it show."

But why should we all have to hide our nerves? The alcohol was giving me a new way to look at the connection. I started to see that real relationships were built on letting some of that fear show.

Suddenly everyone was sharing these honest moments I had always thought were just mine. The beer was not just making me more social. It was making all of us more open.

I reached for my third beer without thinking about it. My hand just knew what to do.

"Look at Davies. Go," Jake said, giving me an approving nod.

Something was shifting inside me. The anxious, overthinking version of myself was still there, but now he was in the background. Out front was someone who could tell a story, make people laugh, and even get attention from Katie.

Katie kept glancing my way. For the first time, I believed I might actually have a chance with her.

The third beer was easier to drink than the first two. Now the edges of the world felt soft and easy. I found myself telling a story about my physics teacher when Jake put his hand on my shoulder.

"Easy, champ. Maybe slow down."

I looked down and realized I already had a fourth beer in my hand. I did not even remember opening it.

"I'm fine," I said, and I meant it. I felt better than fine. I felt like I was finally winning at something that used to defeat me.

Slowing down did not make sense. Why would I stop when everything was going so well? People were laughing. I was being included, and Katie had already asked me three questions about college. It felt like this was what I had been missing all along.

I finished my fourth beer and immediately felt the absence of it. I wanted to hold on to this feeling a little longer.

"I should get another," I said.

"Maybe take a break?" Marcus suggested, but his voice felt far away.

A break from confidence and being included? That felt like the exact wrong move.

I made my way back to the cooler, weaving around groups. As I reached in for another beer, I caught a glimpse of myself in the window. For a moment, I hardly recognized the person looking back. I looked relaxed, smiling easily, moving like I belonged at parties.

I grabbed a fifth beer and walked back, floating on air.

The fifth beer felt like a victory. It seemed like I had finally found the answer to every social problem I ever had. Katie was talking about the stress of college applications, and I nodded along, convinced I understood everything.

"The worst part is writing those essays," she said. "How do you sum up your whole life in just a few hundred words?"

"You pick a single moment that stands for it all," I said, leaning in. "Like this party."

Jake grinned. "This party is your entire life now?"

"This party is when I stopped sitting on the sidelines and started living," I replied. I thought I sounded poetic.

Katie looked at me with something close to admiration. "That's actually beautiful, Dave."

Her words gave me a rush. Suddenly, I wanted to say everything I'd ever felt.

"Katie," I blurted out, "I need to tell you something."

The room faded into the background. I felt like it was just us.

"I've had feelings for you since sophomore year," I said. "You're not just beautiful. You're kind, and smart, and you make everyone feel important."

The words spilled out. In my mind, this kind of honesty had to be right.

Katie's expression changed, but in my beer-fueled state, I thought it meant she was moved. She just looked surprised.

"Dave, you're really drunk right now," she said softly.

Drunk? I shook my head. I was just being honest for once.

"I'm not drunk. I'm telling the truth. I love you. I've loved you for years."

But Katie pulled back, and Jake stood up. I suddenly felt everyone in the room watching us. The laughter and music died down.

"Katie, please," I said, my voice rising. "I know you feel something, too. We have a connection."

Jake stepped in. "Dave, you need to stop."

Stop? I could not stop now. I was so close to finally saying everything.

"I love you," I said, my words echoing in the now-quiet room.

The silence was crushing. Katie's face turned pale, and not in a good way. I realized too late she felt only discomfort and pity.

"Oh, Dave," she said quietly. "You're really drunk. This isn't how this works."

Her words cut through me. I looked around. Every face showed the same thing: embarrassment for me.

"Katie, I—" I started, but Jake gently stepped between us.

"Come on, buddy. Let's get you some water."

I tried to push past him. "Don't call me buddy. This is between me and Katie."

At that moment, I lost my balance and stumbled. It was not a dramatic fall, but it might as well have been.

The spell was broken. People started talking again, quieter this time, and I heard the laughter behind me.

Jake took my arm. "Let's get some water."

I let him lead me to the kitchen, but I kept looking back at Katie, hoping she might understand.

Instead, she was talking to Sarah, both of them looking worried and a little scared.

That was when it hit me. I had ruined everything.

I woke up on Katie's bathroom floor, cheek pressed to the cold tile. My mouth tasted awful, and my head throbbed with pain.

The first thought was confusion—where was I? The second was panic...What had I done?

Sunlight was coming through a small window, so it had to be morning. I realized I must have been out for hours. My memories were scattered and incomplete, like trying to put together a puzzle with half the pieces missing.

I remembered Jake leading me to the kitchen. The taste of water that barely stayed down. Someone telling me to call my parents. Me insisting I could drive home, and everyone pushing back. Then it all got fuzzy. Sitting on the bathroom floor while Jake made a call. Getting sick. Hearing my own voice say things I couldn't remember later.

The truth started to settle in. I had gotten sick at Katie's party. I had told her I loved her in front of everyone. I was now the cautionary tale, the guy everyone would talk about on Monday.

The hangover was bad, but nothing compared to the shame. I couldn't get Katie's face out of my mind...the way she looked at me, not angry, but worried, like she wished she could help.

I managed to sit up, even though the room spun. The mirror showed exactly what I expected: a seventeen-year-old who had made a fool of himself.

My phone was full of missed calls from my parents and messages from Marcus. One text from a number I didn't know made my stomach drop:

"Dave, this is Jake. You're sleeping it off. Your parents think you're at Marcus's. Figure out what you want to tell them. Last night wasn't as bad as you think, but it wasn't great either."

I just wanted to get out without seeing anyone. The front door was twenty feet away. If I could make it, I could hide from everyone for a while.

But I was halfway there when Katie appeared in the kitchen doorway, still in pajamas and holding a cup of coffee.

"Dave," she said softly. "How are you feeling?"

The kindness in her voice stung more than if she had been angry.

"I'm fine," I said, lying. "I was just leaving."

She stepped forward. "Dave, about last night—"

"I don't remember much," I cut in. "I had too much to drink."

"You did," Katie agreed. "But that doesn't mean we shouldn't talk about what you said."

"I shouldn't have said any of it," I muttered. "I was drunk. It didn't mean anything."

But I knew even as I said it, that was not the truth. The feelings were real. The alcohol had just let them out.

"I think it did mean something," Katie said gently. "And I think you're a really sweet guy, Dave. But—"

But. The word that says it all.

"But we're friends," I finished for her. "I know."

She nodded. "Good friends. I don't want this to change that."

I nodded too, forcing myself to look at her. She was being kinder than I deserved.

"It won't change anything," I promised.

Katie smiled. "For what it's worth, you were a lot of fun those first few hours last night. You should let that version of yourself out more often."

That version, the confident and funny one, only seemed to show up when I was drinking.

Monday morning felt like a punishment. I spent all of Sunday in bed, drifting between uneasy sleep and a sense of dread.

The halls at school seemed unfamiliar as I walked to my locker. I saw Katie down the hallway and immediately took a detour to avoid her.

Marcus found me at lunch.

"How are you feeling?" he asked.

"Like I want to change schools," I admitted.

"It really wasn't as bad as you think," Marcus said. "Katie's being kind. She asked me to check on you."

"What did I do after... the big speech?"

Marcus hesitated before answering. "You got emotional. You cried a little. You kept saying you were sorry."

Hearing that was almost worse than not remembering at all.

"But Jake said something interesting," Marcus continued. "He said you were actually pretty cool for most of the night. Before you got too drunk, you were funny and confident."

I remembered that. The first beers had made everything seem possible. For a while, I felt normal.

"Yeah," I said quietly. "It felt like I belonged."

"Maybe you did," Marcus said. "Maybe the alcohol just let you relax and be yourself."

That idea stuck with me for weeks. I thought about the party, not just the embarrassment, but those brief moments when I really connected with people and made them laugh.

I started to notice when I felt that way naturally. Sometimes late at night, when I was tired and less guarded. Other times, when I got so caught up in a conversation or a debate that I forgot to worry about what others thought.

But nothing ever matched how easy it felt in those early hours at Katie's party. Nothing else gave me that same sense of confidence.

I wondered if other people felt like this, too. Maybe that was why alcohol was such a common part of social life. Maybe everyone had their own version of this anxiety.

I began to believe the alcohol was not turning me into someone else, but was actually revealing the real me underneath all the worry.

By graduation, I had managed to fix most of the damage. Katie and I were friendly again. Jake even gave me a nod every now and then, like he respected me. But my view of alcohol had changed. I no longer saw it as something forbidden. I saw it as a tool and a way to access the side of myself I liked.

I promised myself I would be more careful next time. I thought I knew my limits. I thought I understood the risk of going too far, but I also thought I'd learned something valuable about who I could be when I was not fighting myself.

As I packed for MIT that summer, I tucked that lesson away like a secret advantage. I figured college would be a clean slate. And now, I had a formula: just enough alcohol to quiet the anxiety and let my real self show, but not enough to lose control.

It seemed like the perfect plan.

What I did not see then was that I had already started down a path that would cause bigger problems than it solved. The line between using alcohol and needing it was so subtle, I did not realize I had crossed it until many years later, standing in a hotel bathroom with shaking hands.

Back then, I thought I had finally figured out the secret to being the person I wanted to be. The taste of that first beer was already gone, but the feeling it gave me was deeply ingrained in my mind.

I was eighteen, on my way to MIT, with a world of possibilities ahead. And I was already hooked on the idea that there was something out there that could make me into the person I wanted to be. Everything that followed was just me trying to manage a relationship with alcohol that had been broken from the start.

Chapter Three

Functioning Fiction

A FTER THAT NIGHT IN high school, I managed to avoid any serious trouble with drinking for a long time. There were no major embarrassments or obvious problems until much later. For years, it seemed like I had things under control.

The first time it truly hit me, that uneasy suspicion I might have a drinking problem, I was thirty-five, hunched over my desk in a sleek corner office in Midtown Manhattan, riding out a hangover that felt biblical.

Not my first rodeo, obviously. I'd been hungover more times than I cared to count. But this one felt different. Heavier. It had weight. The fluorescent lights above were drilling into my skull like tiny jackhammers. My mind, usually sharp, analytical, and comfortable swimming in complex datasets, was moving like it was stuck in wet cement.

I had three meetings that day, back-to-back. One of them was a major pitch to the executive team. A detailed walkthrough of the predictive model my team had spent months building. The irony was almost funny. I could predict consumer behavior with scary precision. But I couldn't predict. Hell, I couldn't even trust what I would do after a couple of drinks on a regular Tuesday night.

And that's exactly what it had been. Just another Tuesday. No milestone. No crisis. Just a few after-work drinks that somehow unraveled into a 1 a.m. Uber ride I barely remembered and a 6 a.m. wake-up call filled with dread and a tongue that tasted like I'd been licking an ashtray in a dive bar.

"You look terrible," Rachel, my secretary, said as she dropped my third coffee on the desk.

She'd been with me for five years. We didn't need small talk.

"Thanks, Rachel. Feel worse," I grunted.

"Big night?"

I gave a half-hearted nod. Even that movement hurt.

"Haskell's retirement thing?" she asked.

"Yeah," I lied. Haskell's party wasn't until the following week, but that lie rolled out so smoothly, I almost believed it myself.

Rachel gave me a look. Not judgment, just quiet calculation. She didn't buy it, but she was too professional to push. "I'll move your lunch to tomorrow. And I'll grab you some Advil."

As she walked out, I felt it. That low, creeping shame. The same feeling I used to get when I skipped class in college because I'd gone too hard the night before. Except this time, the stakes were higher.

I wasn't a kid anymore. I was a husband, a dad, the head of a team that counted on me.

I pulled up the slide deck and tried to focus. But I couldn't stop thinking about this question that had been scratching at the edge of my mind for months: Why can't I tell when one drink is going to turn into six?

Most people wouldn't have called me a problem drinker. Maybe even the opposite. I didn't drink every day. Hardly ever at home. Just the occasional glass of wine with dinner or a quick scotch while going through emails. I could stop when I had to. I'd done it plenty of times. During my wife's pregnancy, when deadlines piled up, or when I was training for the half-marathon I ran each spring just to prove to myself that I still had control over something.

I wasn't sneaking vodka into coffee mugs or hiding bottles in the linen closet. I drank the way everyone in my world drank: at work functions, industry events, team happy hours. In New York, especially in tech, alcohol was part of the job. If anything, people saw me as the responsible one. I never got sloppy at conferences. Never embarrassed myself in front of clients.

But they didn't see the other nights. The ones I planned around. Nights when I could get sloppy, off the grid, at bars where no one knew my name, with friends who drank like I did. They didn't see how often I went past the limits I swore I'd keep. They didn't see me checking my phone in the mornings, dreading whatever I might have texted. They didn't see the mornings I had to piece the night back together from receipts and fuzzy memories.

The story I told, at work, at home, even to myself, was that I was a high performer who played hard and worked harder. That I could juggle international meetings, tight deadlines, and bedtime stories for my kid. So what if I overdid it sometimes? That was the pressure valve. Not a problem. Just stress management.

That was the fiction I lived inside. And I clung to it, because it was built on all the right cultural scaffolding: ambition, masculinity, high-functioning success. "Real" alcoholics got fired. Got arrested. They missed child support payments and passed out on subway benches. They didn't lead strategy meetings and tuck their kids in at night.

I was just a guy who occasionally had a little too much fun.

At least, that's what I told myself.

Until the morning in my office, when that other narrative, the one I didn't want to hear, started whispering louder.

What if the line between "likes to drink" and "can't stop drinking" isn't as clear as you thought?

Then came a moment I'll never forget.

"Daddy, why are your eyes red?"

It was Sunday morning. We were sitting at the kitchen table. My son Alex, five years old, looked up at me with that wide-eyed curiosity only kids have. I was trying to act like I had the energy to flip pancakes.

"Daddy's just tired," I said, forcing a smile as I poured his orange juice.

My wife, Sarah glanced at me over her coffee. Not mad. Just watching. The night before, I'd gone out with Mark, my college roommate who was in town for a visit. It was supposed to be dinner. We ended up bar-hopping through Williamsburg. I stumbled in at 3 a.m., reeking of whiskey and cigarettes I didn't remember lighting.

"You said you'd be home by eleven," she'd murmured when I crawled into bed.

"Mark only visits once a year," I'd mumbled, like that justified it.

Now, in the bright light of our kitchen, that excuse felt flimsy.

Later, after Alex ran out to play in the backyard, Sarah and I sat at the kitchen island.

"I'm worried about you," she said.

"I'm fine. It was one night."

"It's not just one night. And you know it."

She didn't raise her voice. She didn't need to. Sarah's a pediatric surgeon. She sees what's really going on. She doesn't miss things. It's what made me fall for her.

"It's been happening more often," she said. "The nights out. The hangovers. The broken promises."

I felt myself getting defensive. "I work hard. I'm allowed to let off steam."

She took my hand. "Last month, you missed Alex's preschool play. Last week you bailed on your Singapore call. You said it was food poisoning, but I knew you were still drunk."

I looked at her, and the shame rolled in fast. The truth was, I barely remembered that night. I remembered starting at one bar, then two, then blackout. No idea how I got home.

"I'm handling it," I muttered, pulling my hand away.

"Are you?" she asked. "Because it looks like it's handling you."

I didn't respond. I just sat there, letting her words settle in. I wanted to file this conversation away, like I'd done with so many others.

"It's just a stressful quarter," I said, my go-to line. "Once work settles, I'll cut back."

She didn't argue. She just nodded. After seven years, she knew when I wasn't ready to hear something.

"Alex wants to go to the park this afternoon," she said as she got up. "Think you'll feel up to it?"

Translation: Will you be sober enough to be his dad today?

"Of course," I said, already doing the math, how many hours of sleep, how much Gatorade, how long until I looked okay again.

Once she left the kitchen, I sat there in silence. Head pounding. Mouth dry. And this cold realization forming in my chest:

I was becoming good, too good at living a double life. *The Double Life of a High-Functioning Alcoholic* to be precise.

The guy everyone saw had it all together. But inside, I was fraying. Quietly. Steadily. Losing the thread.

This was the start of a pattern that would stretch on for years. Moments of clarity followed by a fast retreat into denial. Promises to cut back followed by quiet slide-backs into old habits. The fiction would hold. Until it didn't.

And when it finally cracked, it wouldn't just be a bad night. It would be something much bigger.

Chapter Four

The Body Keeps Score

I WAS FORTY-ONE WHEN it happened. The first time my hands started shaking in front of a client. Not just any client, either. This was our biggest one. I was leading their quarterly review, standing at the head of a long conference table, trying to look confident and polished while my body was quietly falling apart.

I'd been out until 3 a.m. the night before. Not because of some big celebration. Just drinks that started after work and somehow kept going. I knew I had an 8:30 meeting. I'd done this dance before. Barely any sleep, way too much coffee, and a smile that said I was fine. I'd gotten good at it. Too good.

But that morning, something felt different. Off.

I reached for my water glass, and that's when it happened. My hand trembled. Just enough to send a little splash over the rim onto the polished table. Barely noticeable in most rooms. But this wasn't most rooms. This was a room full of data analysts, trained to catch the smallest anomaly. The ripple on that water might as well have been a red flare.

"Everything all right, Dave?" Melissa asked, the VP of Analytics for the client. Her eyes were fixed on the glass like it had whispered a secret.

"Absolutely," I said, smiling and setting it down a little too fast. "Too much coffee this morning."

She nodded, but I saw it. The quick sideways glance between her and her team. A recalibration. Nothing dramatic, but I felt it. The first visible crack in what I'd worked so hard to keep together.

I got through the presentation. Not great, but passable. I hit the key points, answered the questions. But I didn't have my usual command, and my team noticed.

After the meeting, Raj pulled me aside. He's my most senior guy. Been with me five years, sharp as hell and loyal. "You okay?" he asked quietly.

"Just tired," I said. The reflex kicked in before he even finished the question.

"You seem more than tired," he said, voice lower now as the last of the client team left the room. "You've seemed... off. For a while."

That stung. Not because he was wrong, but because he saw it. I felt a flash of defensiveness, then fear. Was I really slipping that much? I thought I'd been hiding it.

"I'm fine," I said, picking up my notes and making a show of composure. "Just some family stuff."

That was my other go-to. When "tired" didn't cut it, "family stuff" was vague enough to sound serious, but personal enough to make people back off.

Raj gave me a long look, and then nodded. "Let me know if you need help with anything."

I nodded and left. But as I walked back to my office, I shoved my hands deep into my pockets, trying to ignore the faint tremble still there. I'd felt it before. After long nights, after drinking too much, but never like this. Never in front of people. Never where it could threaten my image.

Once I got back to my office, I did something I'd done before, but with new urgency.

I opened my desk drawer and pulled out the flask I kept for "special occasions." Lately, those occasions were more like emergency landings. Just a sip, I told myself. Just enough to settle the nerves, stop the shaking, clear the fog. Just enough to function.

The whiskey hit fast. My chest warmed. The anxiety backed off. The world came back into focus.

That should have scared the hell out of me.

But it didn't. It felt like control. It felt like proof that I still had this under wraps. I wasn't spiraling. I was managing. I wasn't addicted. I was regulating. That's what I told myself.

I didn't realize it at the time, but my body was trying to send a message, louder and clearer every time. And I was still pretending not to hear it.

The body has its own way of keeping books. It logs every late night, every drink, every time you ignore the warning signs. It doesn't bargain or rationalize like the mind does. It just records. And when the time comes, it sends the bill whether you're ready or not.

By the time I hit my early forties, my body had a full ledger on me. Two decades of heavy drinking weren't just fading memories. They were data points, neatly filed away, and the invoice was starting to show up.

The shaky hands? That was just the first red flag. Then came the heart flutters. Little surges of panic in the middle of the day, like a short circuit in my chest. My heart would stutter or race for no reason. I'd feel a brief wave of dizziness, then it would vanish. Easy to blame on stress or caffeine. Easy to ignore. So I did.

But then the night sweats started. I'd bolt awake at 3 a.m., soaked through, heart pounding like I was being chased. A wave of dread would wash over me, unexplainable, but so familiar it felt routine. Sarah would sometimes wake up and find me changing the sheets like a ghost in the dark.

"You should probably see a doctor," she said one morning after a particularly rough night.

"It's just stress," I muttered. That line had become my blanket excuse. Good for just about anything.

"You've been saying that for months," she said gently. "Maybe it's something else."

I knew exactly what she was hinting at, and I hated it. "I don't have a drinking problem, if that's what you're suggesting."

Sarah didn't snap back. She just let out a long, tired sigh. A sound I'd come to recognize. The sound of someone who's been through this conversation before.

"I didn't say that," she replied. "But alcohol messes with sleep. And you've been drinking more lately. It's not a judgment. It's biology."

She always went back to science. It was her language. And on one level, it was a relief. No guilt. No shame. Just facts. But it also left me exposed. Her words stripped away all my excuses, all the narratives I'd built about being a high-functioning drinker. She wasn't talking about morality. She was talking about systems. About consequences.

And I couldn't deal with that. It made everything too simple.

To me, my drinking wasn't a health issue. It was a lifestyle. A personality trait. A part of how I coped, how I celebrated, how I socialized, how I came down from the edge. It wasn't something I just did. It was something I was. Reducing it to "your body is reacting to too much alcohol" felt like it erased everything I told myself to make it okay.

So I brushed it off. Kept going. Told myself it was work. Parenting. Life. Anything but the one thing it actually was.

And my body? It didn't argue. It just turned up the volume.

The blackouts weren't new. They'd been part of my life for years, sneaking in quietly at first. In my twenties and thirties, they were just part of the territory. Losing the last hour or two of a night out, waking up with a vague sense that I'd missed something but not knowing what. I'd laugh them off. Everyone I drank with had a story like that.

But by the time I hit forty, they were changing, and not in a funny, harmless way. I wasn't just losing the tail end of a night. I was losing entire evenings. I'd wake up in bed or on the couch with no memory of how I got there. No clue what I'd said or done. Just a thick fog where hours used to be.

And that terrified me. Not just the confusion, but the vulnerability of it. That feeling of not knowing. That anything could have happened, and I wouldn't remember a second of it.

Mornings became detective work. I'd scroll through my texts and call logs like I was piecing together a crime scene. Looking for clues. Hoping nothing awful had happened. Praying I hadn't said something I couldn't take back.

Most of the time, what I found wasn't catastrophic. A few late-night texts. A random Uber trip. Conversations I had no recollection of. But sometimes, every so often, there was something. A sharp exchange with Sarah that ended in silence. A message to a colleague that crossed some invisible line of professionalism. Or, worse, a receipt from a bar I didn't even remember walking into.

The worst was the night I apparently got into it with a bartender. Nearly turned physical, according to a horrified text from a colleague who was there. I had zero memory of it. Not even a flicker.

That scared me enough to start Googling.

Are blackouts normal?

What causes memory loss after drinking?

The results were brutal.

"Blackouts are signs of high-risk drinking behavior..."

"Frequent blackouts suggest long-term brain changes..."

"Memory loss episodes are a hallmark of alcohol use disorder..."

I slammed the laptop shut. Nope. Not me. I wasn't that guy. I wasn't some angry drunk in a dive bar picking fights. I was a family man. A department head. Someone who knew how to keep things together.

That incident, I told myself, was a fluke. I hadn't eaten enough. I mixed drinks. It was a one-off.

Except it wasn't.

The bar fights didn't repeat, but the memory gaps did. More often. Deeper. I got more careful about where I drank and who I was with. But no matter how tightly I tried to control it, the blackouts kept coming.

And then one day, I found Sarah's notes.

She had started keeping a record. Quietly. Like a surgeon monitoring a slow, steady decline.

"Feb 10: Dave came home at 2 AM, couldn't remember where he'd been."

"Feb 18: Found Dave passed out on the couch, empty whiskey bottle on the floor."

"March 5: Missed Alex's parent-teacher meeting. Forgot the date after confirming it with me that morning."

Reading it felt like getting punched in the chest. Her handwriting—so neat, so clinical—made it feel undeniable. It wasn't just in my head anymore. There it was, in black and white. A parallel log to the one my body had been keeping all along. And the entries were getting closer together.

The scariest moment came about six months before I finally stopped drinking. I was in Chicago on a business trip, one of those nights where the drinks kept flowing because I was far from home, away from Sarah's watchful eye. It wasn't out of the ordinary. I'd done this routine before: late client dinners, a few too many rounds, stumbling back to the hotel, feeling invincible and slightly buzzed.

But this night was different.

Around 4 a.m., I shot awake in bed. My heart was hammering like it was trying to escape my chest. My whole body was shaking, not just my hands, but my arms, my legs, my core. And I was soaked. The sheets were damp. My T-shirt clung to me, even though the room was cold. I thought I was dying.

But worse than the physical symptoms was this wave, this tidal wave of panic that rolled over me. A full-body sense of doom. Like something terrible was about to happen and there was nothing I could do to stop it.

I couldn't breathe. My vision blurred. My thoughts were racing and collapsing all at once.

I grabbed my phone, ready to call 911. I actually had the number pulled up. And then this terrifying, practical thought snapped through the fog: How am I going to explain this?

To Sarah? To my boss? To the client I was supposed to meet in four hours?

What if they called it what it probably was: alcohol withdrawal?

The shame hit almost as hard as the fear.

So I did what I had to do. What, at that moment, felt like the only way out.

I crawled across the room to the mini-bar. My hands were shaking so badly I could barely twist open the cap on one of those tiny vodka bottles. I downed it. Then another. And I sat on the cold tile floor of the bathroom, back against the wall, waiting.

Within twenty minutes, the storm started to calm. My heart slowed. My hands steadied. The dread backed off just enough to think straight again.

And that's when the truth hit me. Not as a whisper or a warning, but like a door slamming open: my body needed alcohol just to function. This wasn't about stress or a bad night's sleep. This wasn't dehydration or poor planning.

This was dependency. Raw and undeniable.

I wish I could say that the realization changed everything. That I went home and told Sarah. That I got help.

But I didn't.

I made rules instead. New boundaries I was sure I could stick to. No more than three drinks. Water between rounds. No drinking two nights in a row. No hard liquor on business trips.

I clung to those rules like they were life rafts.

They lasted maybe two weeks.

Eventually, one drink turned into four again. The rules got bent, then broken. And every time I got through another dinner or happy hour without shaking or blacking out, I convinced myself that night in Chicago had been a fluke. A one-off. A bad combination of alcohol and jet lag.

The memory faded. Not completely, but just enough to quiet the fear. Just enough to let me keep going.

Because the truth is, the mind can ignore almost anything if it's not ready to face what it knows deep down is true.

"Have you noticed your father's hands shaking in the morning?"

Sarah asked the question like she was commenting on the weather. Calm, almost casual. We were sitting on the couch after putting Alex to bed, a documentary playing quietly in the background while we both zoned out in separate thoughts. Her voice cut through the quiet, and I felt it like a jab to the ribs.

"What? No. Why would you say that?"

"Because I have," she said. "And so has Alex."

That last part hit harder than anything. My son? Noticing?

"What are you talking about?"

"Last weekend," she said, still calm. "You were making pancakes, and later Alex asked me why your hands were 'doing the wiggles.' That's what he called it."

Shame flushed over me. Fast, hot, dizzying. "I was just tired. You know I haven't been sleeping well."

Sarah turned to face me fully. Her expression wasn't angry. It was the same one I'd seen her give anxious parents at the hospital when she had to deliver hard news. Gentle. Steady. Measured.

"Dave, I'm a doctor," she said softly. "I know alcohol withdrawal when I see it."

"Withdrawal?" I practically shouted. "Come on, that's ridiculous. You have to be an alcoholic to go through withdrawal."

"That's not actually true," she said, maddeningly composed. "Physical dependency isn't all or nothing. It builds over time. You don't have to be drinking a bottle of vodka a day to start having symptoms."

"I don't have withdrawal symptoms," I said. Flat. Automatic.

She didn't flinch. "You have tremors in the morning that disappear after your first drink. You sweat through the sheets at night. You get anxious and irritated when you haven't had a drink in a while. You're edgy when we go places where drinking isn't an option. Those are textbook early withdrawal signs."

She wasn't judging. She was stating facts. That was what made it worse. She wasn't even emotional. Just clear-eyed and calm, like she was going down a chart.

I couldn't argue with what she said, so I attacked how she said it. "Are you diagnosing me now? Using your medical training to analyze normal stress responses?"

Sarah didn't take the bait.

"I'm not diagnosing you," she said. "I'm telling you what I see as someone who loves you. And I'm telling you that our six-year-old is seeing it too."

That landed like a punch to the stomach. Alex. I could lie to myself about how my drinking affected me. I could even convince myself Sarah was strong enough to handle it. But my son? Knowing? Noticing? That shattered something.

"I'll cut back," I said quietly, reaching for the line I'd used more times than I could count.

Sarah didn't answer right away. When she finally spoke, her voice was gentle but firm. "I think we're past that, Dave. I think you need help."

"I don't need help," I said reflexively. "I just need more discipline."

She shook her head. "You're one of the most disciplined people I know. At work, with your workouts, with everything else. If this was about discipline, don't you think you'd have fixed it by now?"

I didn't have a response to that. Because it was true.

"It's different," I muttered.

"Yes," she said. "It is. That's what I've been trying to tell you. This isn't about willpower. Your body is dependent. It's been trying to tell you for years. And now it's screaming."

I wanted to fight her on it. I wanted to push back, insist that I was still in control. But I was so damn tired. Tired of the hiding, the managing, the endless inner bargaining about when and how and how much I could drink. Tired of pretending I didn't feel the fear building every time my body gave me another warning sign.

"I'll think about it," I finally said. It wasn't a promise. It wasn't even a decision. But it was the first time I hadn't outright denied the truth.

She nodded and gently squeezed my hand. Then we both turned back to the screen, though neither of us was really watching.

We sat there, side by side, each lost in our own version of what came next. I imagine Sarah was picturing a real shift. A plan, a path to sobriety, maybe therapy, maybe support groups. I was calculating the bare minimum I could change to make her feel reassured without having to give up the one thing I still clung to. The one thing I still thought made me whole.

What neither of us knew was that my body was preparing one last warning. A moment so clear, so terrifying, that even I wouldn't be able to explain it away.

But that moment hadn't come yet.

That night, I just sat there, quiet on the outside and in turmoil on the inside. Wondering if she might be right. Wondering if this thing I kept calling a "choice" was actually a condition. A process. A progression with a finish line I was fast approaching.

It was the closest I'd come to facing it. The truth that had been tapping at my shoulder for years. My body was keeping score. And whether I admitted it or not, I was running out of time.

Chapter Five

The Moments We Pretend to Forget

"DAD, DO YOU REMEMBER when you fell at Uncle Mike's wedding?"

The question came out of nowhere. Alex and I were sitting at the kitchen table, working through his math homework. He was five then. I was forty-three, just over a year away from my last drink. I remember my hand freezing midair, pencil hovering above a half-finished multiplication problem.

"What do you mean, buddy?" I asked, trying to keep my voice light.

"At the wedding," he said. "You fell down when everyone was dancing, and Mom had to help you get up. Don't you remember?"

I didn't.

I remembered the ceremony. The vineyard. The great food. The wine. I remembered the start of the reception, laughing with my in-laws, clinking glasses, dancing to the first few songs. And then, fog. I'd assumed I'd just gotten tipsy and had a good time. Apparently, I'd had a very good time.

"Oh, that," I said, stalling. "I must've tripped on something."

Alex squinted at me, unconvinced. Kids have this radar for when adults aren't telling the whole truth.

"Mom said you had too much happy juice."

I blinked. "Happy juice?"

"Yeah," he said. "She said sometimes grown-ups drink too much happy juice and then they act silly. Like fall-down silly."

I made a mental note to talk to Sarah later. But in that moment, all I could think about was what my son had seen. What else had he noticed? What else had I done that I couldn't remember?

"Well," I said slowly, "Mom's right. Sometimes adults drink more than they should. And I'm sorry you saw that. That probably felt kind of weird, huh?"

Alex shrugged like it wasn't a big deal. "It wasn't scary. Just weird. You were acting different. Not like you."

Not like you.

That landed harder than anything else. Because he was right. When I drank too much and when I slipped into those gaps, I couldn't remember. I wasn't me. Or maybe I was a version of me I didn't want to admit existed.

"Let's get back to these math problems," I said, my voice too cheerful, too forced.

Later that night, after Alex was asleep, I found Sarah in our bedroom, reading.

"Did you really tell him I had too much happy juice at Mike's wedding?"

She looked up, calm. "Yeah. He asked what was wrong. I had to tell him something."

"You could've said I tripped."

"He wouldn't have bought it," she said flatly. "You were visibly drunk, Dave. You knocked over a centerpiece, then fell, tried to get up, and fell again. It wasn't exactly subtle."

I felt shame settle over me like a heavy coat.

"I don't remember any of that."

"I know," she said softly. "That's part of the problem."

I sat on the edge of the bed, the weight of it hitting me all at once. "What else happened?"

She set her book down. "You gave a long, rambling toast that didn't really make sense. You got into an argument with the bartender when he cut you off. And you told Mike's new mother-in-law that her dress made her look like a 'fancy lampshade."

I buried my face in my hands. "Jesus."

Sarah wasn't trying to humiliate me. She was just recounting facts. But they landed like body blows.

"The thing is," she continued, "this isn't a one-off anymore. It's happening more often. What used to be once or twice a year is now every few weeks. And people are starting to notice. Not just me. Not just Alex. Everyone."

I wanted to argue. I wanted to tell her she was exaggerating, that these were isolated moments strung together unfairly. But I couldn't. The gaps in my memory were becoming more frequent. The stories, like this one, kept coming back to me from other people. Not from my own recollection.

"I'm sorry," I said, though it didn't feel like enough.

"I don't need you to be sorry," Sarah said. "I need you to get help. Before Alex has too many memories like this. Before it becomes what he thinks is normal."

I nodded. Not because I was ready to change, but because I couldn't deny the truth of what she'd said.

Our son was watching. Taking notes. Building his idea of what it meant to be a man, a father, an adult. And right now, what he saw was someone unpredictable. Someone who disappeared into himself after too many drinks. Someone who fell down at weddings and couldn't explain it the next day.

It was a sobering realization but not, as it turned out, sobering enough.

That would come later.

It would take another moment, more public, more humiliating, before I could finally admit just how much of myself I'd been losing. And just how much my son had already seen.

The moments we try hardest to forget are often the ones other people remember in perfect detail. That mismatch between our hazy version and their sharp memory creates this strange kind of social dissonance. You're left second-guessing yourself. Did it really happen that way? Was it that bad?

By the time I reached my early forties, I had a whole collection of these blurred-out moments. Nights I thought had been fun, harmless, even forgettable, but that other people remembered vividly. And not in a good way.

Take the holiday party where I apparently got into a heated political debate with my boss's spouse. I had no memory of it. None. A colleague brought it up weeks later, laughing it off like it was just another "Dave moment." I laughed too, pretending to remember.

Or the happy hour where I told one of our junior data scientists that her boyfriend "sounded like a total loser." It wasn't a thought I would have ever said out loud while sober, but there it was, served back to me later in someone else's retelling.

Or the neighborhood block party where I fell asleep in a lawn chair. Not in my own yard, mind you. On someone else's property. They had to wake me up when the party was over. The story made its way around the neighborhood, always told with a chuckle. But underneath the laughter, I could feel the awkward pause. The unspoken, Is he okay?

What tied all these moments together was the same sinking pattern: I didn't remember them. I only knew about them through secondhand stories. And when I heard them, I felt that particular kind of shame. The one you try to laugh through, but that leaves a pit in your stomach afterward.

Still, I had a way of smoothing it over. I had lines ready.

"Classic Dave, always the life of the party!"

"You know how I get when I'm passionate about something."

"Long week. A few beers. The sun must've done me in."

One excuse might have passed. Two, maybe. But stacked together, they were saying something I didn't want to hear. Something I wasn't ready to admit.

They weren't funny stories. They were warning signs.

And I kept waving them off, even as the list grew longer.

The cracks were starting to show at work, and no matter how hard I tried to patch them, I could feel the pressure building underneath.

For a long time, I'd managed to maintain a reputation as a sharp, driven, occasionally moody leader. The kind of guy whose quirks were tolerated because the results spoke for themselves. But that version of me was getting harder to maintain. The stories were starting to stack up.

There was the Monday morning executive meeting where I showed up still a little buzzed from the night before. I didn't realize it until halfway through, when the CFO leaned over and said I had a "unique perspective" on our quarterly numbers. It was a polite way of saying I wasn't making sense.

Then there was the client dinner where I told the same story three times. Not once. Three times. My team didn't say anything at the moment. They were too polite, but the next day, someone gently brought it up during our debrief, in that careful tone people use when they're trying not to embarrass you.

Or the performance review I gave where I completely contradicted something I'd told that team member the week before. She was gracious about it. She acted like I'd simply changed my mind. But I hadn't. I'd just forgotten.

The most unsettling shift, though, came from Raj.

He'd been with me for years. Smart, loyal, reliable. He was the guy I trusted to keep the engine running when I was pulled in five different directions. And lately, I could tell he was changing the way he worked with me.

He started double-checking our decisions. Looping others into conversations that used to stay between the two of us. Sending follow-up emails that felt like receipts, little logs of what we'd discussed, just in case.

He was covering for me.

When I finally asked him about it, I tried to sound curious, not threatened. "Hey, I've noticed you're taking more of a lead with the client accounts. Everything okay?"

He gave me a careful smile. "Just trying to provide more consistent coverage for the team."

My stomach dropped. "You don't think I'm being consistent?"

There was a pause. A beat too long.

"I think you've got a lot on your plate," he said. "And it makes sense to build some redundancy into our client relationships."

Redundancy. That word hit like a slap. It was corporate-speak, sure. But I knew exactly what he meant. So did he.

I repeated it. "Redundancy."

He nodded. "Yes."

It was the most professional way he could say what we both knew: that my reliability had slipped, that my behavior had become unpredictable, and that he was quietly building a safety net in case I couldn't hold it together.

I should have been grateful. Raj was being loyal, discreet, respectful. He wasn't throwing me under the bus. He was trying to protect me.

But I didn't feel grateful. I felt exposed.

And afraid.

If Raj had noticed, who else had? What were they saying when I wasn't in the room? Were they covering for me too? Whispering about me? Watching for the next slip?

I'd spent my whole career building a reputation: steady, brilliant, capable. That identity had taken years to forge. And now, it felt like it was cracking around the edges.

The thing that scared me most wasn't the shaking hands or the night sweats or even the memory gaps. It was the realization that once people started to see you differently, you couldn't put that version of yourself back in the box.

The narrative had begun to shift.

Not "Dave is brilliant but intense."

Now it was "Dave might have a problem."

The social slip-ups were embarrassing, sure. But they usually stayed within their own little bubbles. Work people, friends, neighbors. I could compartmentalize them, pretend they were isolated. What really scared me were the moments that crossed boundaries, the ones that let my drinking bleed into every corner of my life at once.

Like the school fundraiser.

It was a well-dressed evening in the gym-turned-ballroom, filled with parents, teachers, and staff. I'd had a few too many glasses of wine. Just enough to feel chatty, generous, a little unstoppable.

When the auction began, I got swept up in the energy, raising my paddle over and over, determined to win the most impressive item on the list: a weekend getaway at a boutique hotel in the Berkshires.

I won. Spent nearly ten grand. For a package probably worth half that.

Financially, we could handle it. That wasn't the issue. But the way I acted, the way I kept bidding, laughing loudly, calling it "our little revenge vacation," was less about charity and more about being seen. I became the spectacle that night. And it didn't take long for the whispers to start.

The following week, during school pickup, another parent approached me, someone I barely knew, but who smiled like we were old friends.

"Hey, Dave. Are you and Sarah okay... financially?"

I blinked, caught off guard. "Yeah, totally fine," I said, forcing a laugh. "Just got a little competitive with the bidding. It's all for a good cause, right?"

She nodded, hesitantly. "Right. It's just... you seemed really enthusiastic."

"That's me," I said, too brightly. "Mr. Enthusiasm."

Then I changed the subject to the upcoming science fair and walked away feeling hollow.

Later that night, Sarah told me one of her colleagues (whose kid also goes to Alex's school) had asked if I was "doing all right."

"What did you say?" I asked, already bracing for the answer.

"I told her you were under a lot of pressure at work," she said. Her voice was flat. Her eyes said everything else.

"Thank you," I said quietly.

"Don't thank me," she replied, sharper now. "I'm not doing you any favors by covering for you. I'm just trying to protect Alex and myself from the fallout."

I didn't respond. Because what could I say? She was right.

Sarah hadn't signed up to play damage control. She hadn't volunteered to step in and make excuses when I slipped up in public. But that's what she'd been doing, more and more. Not because she wanted to. Because she had to.

She was becoming collateral damage in a problem I still wasn't ready to call what it was.

The hardest memories, the ones I still flinch from, are the ones that involved Alex. Not the public embarrassments or the work missteps. The ones where my drinking didn't just hurt me. It let him down.

Like the bedtime stories that never happened because I passed out on the couch. Or the Saturday morning sports practices I showed up to wearing sunglasses and clutching a travel mug filled with "coffee" that was really half whiskey. Just enough to stop my hands from shaking, enough to make me feel functional again.

Or the promises. God, the promises. So many of them made in good spirits, broken in silence.

"You said we'd go to the science museum today," Alex said one Sunday morning. He was already dressed, ready to go, excitement in his eyes.

I stared at him, blank. I had no memory of that plan. The night before was another blur: dinner, drinks, more drinks after that, then the couch. My head throbbed, and the thought of loud crowds and bright lights made me nauseous.

"I'm not feeling great, buddy," I said, trying to sound casual, like this was a random flu instead of the result of pouring too much into myself the night before. "Can we go next weekend instead?"

He didn't get mad. He didn't even look surprised. Just disappointed. Quietly, deeply disappointed. And that was worse.

"Okay," he said, and walked away to tell Sarah.

Later, in the kitchen, Sarah cornered me. Her voice was low, controlled, but sharp.

"That's the third time this month you've bailed on him."

"I know," I said. "I feel awful."

"It's not about how you feel," she snapped. "It's about what you're teaching him to expect from you. From men."

That hit a nerve. My own dad had been solid. Dependable to the core. He showed up for everything: games, plays, parent-teacher conferences. I never had to wonder if he'd be there. His consistency had been the ground I stood on. It let me believe the world was safe.

What was I giving Alex?

"I'll make it up to him," I said.

Sarah just shook her head. "That's what you always say. But you can't make up for these moments. They're gone. And what stays with him is the pattern. That Dad says one thing and does another. That he makes promises when he's feeling good and breaks them when he's hungover."

She wasn't trying to be cruel. She was telling me the truth.

And I had no comeback. No justification that didn't sound hollow.

Because she was right.

I was failing at the most important job I had: being the dad my son could count on.

And still, even knowing that, I didn't stop. I meant it when I said I'd do better. I always did. I'd cut back, drink less, white-knuckle my way through a few dry weeks. But it never stuck. Sooner or later, I'd slide back into the same routines.

The gap between who I believed I was, a devoted father, a capable professional, a husband who loved his family, and who I actually was becoming, was getting harder to ignore. The dissonance was exhausting.

Something had to give. Either I'd have to let go of the image I had of myself, or I'd have to finally change. Really change.

I just didn't know yet which it would be.

The moment everything changed didn't happen at a bar, or on a bender, or even alone. It happened at my son's school camping trip.

Alex was five. It was an annual father-child weekend, a tradition at his school. A couple of days in the Catskills: hiking, fishing, campfires, s'mores. A chance to bond, unplug, and, in my case, maybe try to redeem myself a little after too many missed promises and half-kept commitments.

I'd been looking forward to it. Really looking forward to it. I bought new gear, packed for both of us, and told myself firmly that I wouldn't drink. Or if I did, maybe just a single beer by the fire once Alex was asleep. Nothing that would derail things.

That plan didn't last the first night.

We hiked. We grilled hot dogs. We did the whole rustic dad-and-son routine. And once the kids were zipped into their tents, the dads circled the main fire. That's when someone pulled out a bottle of good bourbon, and the cups started going around.

"Just one," I thought, accepting the cup. "Be social. Be normal."

But one became two. Then a few more. The fire got warmer, the talk looser. I wasn't the only one drinking, but I was the only one who kept going.

I don't remember everything. I've pieced most of it together from what people told me later.

Apparently, I got loud. Held court on politics. Rambled about parenting like I was giving a TED Talk. When people tried to quiet me, "Hey, the kids are sleeping," I waved them off.

"They can't hear us!" I reportedly shouted. We were surrounded by tents. Of course they could.

Then, for reasons I still don't fully understand, I decided I needed to check on Alex.

I stumbled through the dark, shining my flashlight into random tents, calling his name. I woke up other kids. One of the organizers stepped in.

"Mr. Halston, please," he said gently. "The kids are sleeping."

"I need to see my son," I insisted. Belligerent, slurring, making a scene.

At some point I tripped and fell on a tent, ripping it open. That's when Alex came out. Sleepy, confused, scared. He saw two other dads trying to steady me as I argued with them, barely able to stand.

That image, my son watching his father act like a drunk stranger, is burned into my memory, even though most of the night isn't.

I woke up the next morning in our tent. Alone. Head pounding. Alex was gone.

He'd eaten breakfast with another dad, his friend's father, who stepped in because I couldn't. When I walked out into the clearing, the other parents were polite in the way people are when they don't want to say what they're really thinking. They kept their distance. Some kept their kids away from me altogether.

One of the organizers, also a school board member, pulled me aside. His tone was quiet but firm.

"You're welcome to stay for the rest of the trip," he said, "but you need to stay completely sober. We can't have a repeat of last night. Not around the kids."

The shame was crushing. My hangover didn't even compare. I'd embarrassed myself, sure, but far worse, I'd embarrassed my son. I'd made him afraid. And I'd done it in front of his school community: fathers, teachers, friends.

When Alex came up to me that afternoon, he looked hesitant. His first words shattered me.

"Are you better now?"

Not "Are you okay?" Not "What happened?" Just a quiet, careful scan: Are you yourself again? Are you safe?

"Yeah, buddy," I said. "I'm better. And I'm so sorry about last night."

He nodded. "Mr. Jensen let me have breakfast with them. He made blueberry pancakes."

"That was nice of him."

"Yeah." He looked down, kicked at the dirt. Then he asked, just like that, "Dad, are you an alcoholic? Tyler says his uncle is an alcoholic and sometimes he acts scary like you did."

It felt like a punch to the gut.

My first instinct was to protect him and myself. "No, buddy," I said. "I just drank too much last night. It was a mistake."

But even as I said it, I knew it wasn't good enough. The label didn't matter as much as what my drinking was doing to me, to him, to our relationship. This wasn't just about definitions anymore.

The rest of the weekend passed in a blur of forced sobriety and quiet damage control. I went through the motions: hiking, fishing, sitting by the fire, trying to rebuild something with Alex, trying to seem normal to the other dads. But I knew something had changed.

I had crossed a line. This wasn't just a private problem anymore. I had turned it into a public spectacle. I wasn't the high-functioning guy who drank a little too much sometimes. I was the dad who had to be watched.

On the drive home, Alex fell asleep in the back seat. I drove in silence, hearing his question echo in my mind.

Are you an alcoholic?

For the first time, I didn't dismiss it. I didn't reach for the usual excuses. I just sat with it.

Maybe I didn't drink every day. Maybe I hadn't lost my job. Maybe I didn't fit the stereotype. But alcohol had started running my life. It was changing how I saw myself. Worse, it was changing how my son saw me.

I didn't make any big promises that day. I didn't declare I was done. But a door cracked open, just enough for honesty to start slipping through.

Later, when I told Sarah a watered-down version of what happened, she didn't push. She just looked at me and said, "Are you ready to talk about getting help?"

"Not yet," I said. "But I'm starting to think I might need to."

It was a small sentence. But for someone who'd spent years buried in denial, it was a shift as big as a landslide.

The camping trip didn't fix anything. But it was the beginning of the end. The moment I started seeing my drinking for what it really was. Not a habit, not a stress reliever, but a problem that was breaking things I cared about.

Especially the little boy asleep in the back seat.

Chapter Six

The First Thirty Days: Breaking the Spell

PEOPLE ALWAYS ASK ME, "When did you know you had to quit drinking?" Like there was a single moment, some cinematic rock bottom that snapped everything into focus. I wish it were that simple. The truth was messier. It wasn't one moment. It was dozens. All of them small alarms I silenced or snoozed until, finally, I couldn't.

If I had to pick a moment where denial truly became impossible, it was a random Tuesday morning in March. 2:37 a.m. to be exact. I was on the bathroom floor of our Brooklyn brownstone, curled up against the side of the tub. My heart was racing like it wanted out of my chest, my hands and arms shaking so violently I could barely breathe, and this crushing sense of doom had taken over. Not panic. Not anxiety. Doom. Like I was dying.

Sarah found me on the bathroom floor, curled up like I'd been dropped there. I must have made a noise, or maybe she just has that sixth sense after years of hospital nights. Either way, she was beside me, half-awake, reaching for my wrist to check my pulse.

"I think I'm having a heart attack," I gasped. The words barely made it out. My chest thudded. My arms were shaking so badly I could hardly keep them pressed to my side.

She felt my forehead and peered into my eyes, her face tight with concern. "How much did you drink?" she asked, voice low, almost distracted as she tried to sort through symptoms.

"Not that much," I insisted. "A few after work, that's it. I stopped hours ago. I..." My words tripped over themselves. "This can't be happening because of that."

She stayed quiet for a moment, just looking at me. Then she let out a breath, not angry, just tired. "We should go to the ER," she said. "Your heart's racing. You're sweating through your shirt. This isn't normal."

I shook my head, the panic rising for a different reason now. "No hospitals," I said, almost pleading. "It'll show up on my record. I just need... I don't know, something to make this stop."

For a long moment she just watched me. I could feel her weighing all the things she wanted to say, and all the times she'd tried to say them before. She kneeled a little closer. "You're not okay, Dave," she said, her voice softer now. "Whatever you think this is, your body's trying to tell you something."

I couldn't look at her. In that moment, all I could focus on was the shivering in my arms, the hammer in my chest, and the realization creeping in, undeniable and slow. I wasn't in control anymore. My body was calling the shots.

"Can you help me?" I asked. "Please."

"I'm a pediatric surgeon," she said. "Not an addiction specialist. But I'll get you through this tonight. That's all I can promise."

She came back with water, Gatorade, and two leftover Ativan from a flight anxiety prescription. "This will calm your system. But it's just a patch. You need real help, Dave. This isn't sustainable."

As the medication took hold and the shakes slowly faded, something else surfaced: clarity.

This was it. I wasn't just someone who occasionally overdid it. My body needed alcohol now. Without it, it rebelled. It collapsed. The idea that I was in control had been a fantasy. I wasn't choosing to drink anymore. I was avoiding withdrawal.

"I need to stop drinking," I said, the words feeling strange and heavy in my mouth.

Sarah nodded. "Yes. You do."

"I don't know how," I admitted, and suddenly I was crying. Really crying. Years of pressure and shame cracking open in one sentence.

She took my hand. "We'll figure it out."

That night marked the end of my long game of pretend. I couldn't deny it anymore. I wasn't a guy who liked to drink. I was a guy who needed to. And that need was destroying me from the inside out.

The next morning, still shaky but clearer than I'd felt in ages, I called in sick to work. Then I did something I'd never done: I googled what happens when you stop drinking after years of heavy use.

What I found scared me. Withdrawal can be dangerous, even deadly. The symptoms can last for weeks. The psychological roller coaster? Months. Maybe longer. Words like "PAWS" (post-acute withdrawal syndrome) and "kindling effect" became part of my vocabulary.

What shook me the most was realizing that my experience in the bathroom wasn't some exaggerated response. It was textbook withdrawal. According to the clinical scales, I wasn't "borderline." I was solidly in the "moderate-to-severe alcohol use disorder" range.

When Sarah got back from dropping off Alex, I showed her what I'd read. "Is this really where I'm at?" I asked, hoping for some reassurance.

She didn't sugarcoat it. "Yes. I've suspected this for a long time. But the last year and a half, it's been clear."

"Why didn't you say something sooner?"

"I did," she said, calm but firm. "You just weren't ready to hear it."

She was right. I had deflected, downplayed, promised moderation that never lasted. The camping trip? That was just the latest in a long string of incidents she had tried to get me to see for what they were.

"So... what do I do now?" I asked.

Sarah looked at me with that steady gaze of hers. "You've got options. Inpatient. Outpatient. Groups. Therapy. Medication. But none of that matters until you answer one question. Do you want to quit completely, or are you still hoping to manage it?"

The question knocked the wind out of me. Even after everything, even after shaking on the bathroom floor, I realized part of me was still clinging to the idea that maybe, just maybe, I could keep drinking in a controlled way.

"I don't know," I said.

"Then that's your first task," she replied. "Because everything else depends on your answer."

And that's where it started, not with a dramatic goodbye to alcohol, but with an honest look at how deep I was in. Not with certainty, but with something close to it: the willingness to finally stop lying to myself.

I didn't drink that day. Or the next. Not because of some bold resolution or sweeping vow to change. I stayed sober because my body was wrecked, rattled from the withdrawal, terrified of slipping into another episode like the one on the bathroom floor. For those first 48 hours, sobriety wasn't a choice. It was survival.

I told no one, apart from Sarah. I called in sick to work, claimed it was a stomach virus, and holed up at home. I avoided texts, skipped video calls, stayed off Slack. The truth was, I wasn't ready for anyone to notice a change. I wasn't ready to call myself someone who didn't drink. Hell, I wasn't even sure this was a permanent thing.

By the third day, my body had settled. No more shaking. No more crushing dread. But emotionally, I felt fragile, like I was walking around without skin. Going back to the office felt impossible. Not because of the work, but because of everything around it. The happy hours. The client drinks. The casual "Want to grab a beer?" that floated through the week like clockwork.

And that's when I realized I had to decide: Was I taking a break, or was I actually quitting?

Sarah's question, moderation or abstinence, kept echoing in my mind. Moderation sounded nice. Clean. Manageable. No big declarations. I'd just drink less. Smarter. Only at social events. Only wine. Or just weekends. Maybe three drinks, max.

But when I looked back honestly, every moderation plan I'd ever made had failed. Not once. Not occasionally. Every single time. I'd start with rules, and within weeks, those rules would bend. Then break. Then vanish.

That night, after Alex went to bed, I sat in our home office with my laptop and started digging into the science behind moderation versus abstinence. It was sobering. Literally.

Everything I read pointed in the same direction: for people who have crossed a certain threshold with alcohol, especially those who have experienced withdrawal, moderation almost never works. The brain changes. The body adapts. And the idea of "controlled drinking" becomes a myth we cling to out of fear.

At midnight, I closed the laptop and sat there, staring into the dark.

Moderation was off the table.

I didn't say the words out loud, but I felt the shift. It was like watching a drawbridge lift between two parts of your life and knowing you're never going back across.

The next morning, while Alex got dressed for school, I poured coffee and told Sarah.

"I need to stop completely," I said. "Not just take a break. I mean, I need to stop for good."

She looked at me. Not shocked. Not triumphant. Just steady. "I think that's the right choice," she said. "How do you want to start?"

"I don't know," I admitted. "I can't disappear for a month. I can't do residential treatment. I've got work. And I don't want to be away from you and Alex."

"There are other ways," she said. "Outpatient programs. Recovery groups. Even doctors who specialize in addiction and can help with meds, if you want that."

The way she said it made all the difference. Calm. Clinical. Like this was a health problem with real solutions. Not a moral failure or a shameful secret.

"I'll look into options today," I promised.

Then she asked the question I'd been dreading. "What are you going to say at work?"

That one stopped me.

Because quitting drinking publicly meant admitting I had a problem. And professionally, that scared the hell out of me. Would clients still trust me? Would my team still see me as capable? What if word got out? I wasn't ready for that kind of vulnerability, not yet.

"I think I'll just say I'm on a health kick," I said. "Training for a marathon or something."

Sarah raised an eyebrow. "Okay," she said slowly. "But just remember. Secrets take energy to maintain. You might need that energy for recovery."

She was right. But I wasn't there yet. I needed a story, even a fake one, to keep me moving forward without unraveling.

As we packed up breakfast and Alex shouted for help with his backpack, Sarah paused at the door.

"I'm proud of you," she said. "I know this isn't easy."

Her words hit me harder than I expected. I'd braced for a lecture, or a sigh, or a "finally." Instead, she gave me grace.

"I'm scared," I said, the words catching in my throat.

"I know," she replied. "But you've done hard things before. And this time, you're not doing it alone."

It wasn't dramatic. There was no swelling music, no grand goodbye to booze. Just two people in a kitchen, starting a hard thing together.

But it was enough.

Day four without drinking brought my first real test: a client dinner. The kind of event where drinks aren't just expected, they're part of the job. I'd considered backing out, claiming a scheduling conflict or a stomach bug, but I knew I couldn't keep dodging these situations. If I was going to live differently, I had to learn how to show up in the world without a drink in my hand.

So I made a plan. I'd stick to club soda with lime. If anyone asked, I'd say I was taking a break from drinking for health reasons. Maybe mention a half-marathon I was "training" for. Keep it simple. Keep the focus on business.

It all sounded good in theory.

Then I walked into the steakhouse, and the client, a CEO who's practically a connoisseur of top-shelf whiskey, greeted me with,

"You've got to try this new single malt I just discovered. It's incredible."

I smiled, heart racing a little. "Actually, I'm not drinking right now. Training for a half-marathon."

He paused, eyebrows raised but only for a second. "Good for you. Discipline. I respect that."

And just like that, it passed. No big scene. No interrogation. But still, I felt exposed. Like I'd peeled back something private and handed it to him without meaning to. It was just a drink I turned down, but somehow it felt bigger than that.

The night rolled on. My colleague and the client ordered rounds of drinks. I stuck to my soda. On the surface, everything was normal. I made my points, closed the loop on some negotiations, even had a few good laughs.

But underneath it, I felt separate. Like I was sitting behind a pane of glass, watching everyone else ease into the soft blur of alcohol while I stayed sharp and awkwardly present.

Two things caught me off guard.

First, being sober gave me an edge. I caught subtleties in the conversation that I might have missed before, the hesitation in a tone, the real reason behind a strategic shift. I was fully there, and sharper than I expected to be.

Second, the cravings weren't subtle. They weren't gentle. They were loud and physical. My body wanted a drink the way it used to want water after a run. I didn't expect that. It wasn't like giving up sugar or skipping a second coffee. It felt more primal than that.

When I got home, Sarah was waiting.

"How was it?" she asked.

"I didn't drink," I said. Saying it out loud made the whole evening feel real. I'd done it. A small win. But my voice gave me away.

She tilted her head. "But?"

"But it was hard. Really hard. Physically uncomfortable. And socially... strange. I felt like I didn't belong. Like I was on the outside looking in."

Sarah nodded. "That makes sense. Your brain's still adjusting. And you're shifting your entire social identity. That takes time."

I rubbed my eyes. "How much time are we talking about?"

"The physical stuff? A week or two, usually. But the emotional side, the cravings, the awkwardness, the self-image stuff, that can take months. Sometimes longer."

"Years?" I asked, already exhausted by the idea.

"Not years of feeling like this," she said quickly. "But years of building something new. A new rhythm, a new way of connecting, a new way of being. Like learning a language. It's clunky and self-conscious at first. But eventually, it gets smoother. You stop thinking about it."

I let that sink in.

She wasn't sugarcoating it. She wasn't giving me a pep talk. Just telling the truth.

And somehow, that helped.

This wasn't a failure. It was the beginning of the process. I was just in the part that hurt. The messy, itchy, awkward part where everything felt foreign and fragile.

It wouldn't always feel like that.

But for now, I had made it through day four. Sober. Unsteady. But still standing.

The first two weeks without alcohol hit me harder than I expected. I'd read about the symptoms: insomnia, mood swings, cravings, but reading about something and living it are two very different things.

Sleep was a mess. Either I couldn't fall asleep, or I'd wake up at 3 a.m. and just lie there, mind racing. During the day, I felt like I was moving through molasses: foggy, tired, irritable. I snapped at Alex over something trivial. Barked at a teammate during a strategy session because I misread his tone. Even lost my train of thought during a big presentation, which had never happened before. I was used to being sharp, quick, in control. Suddenly I felt like I was glitching in real time.

And I couldn't help but wonder: Was I doing more damage by not drinking? Was this new sober version of me, distracted, emotional, tense, really an upgrade?

The temptation crept in almost every day. Just one drink, I'd tell myself. Just to level things out. Just to sleep. Just to make the edge a little less sharp.

But then I'd remember that night in the bathroom. The shaking. The panic. Sarah's voice telling me this wasn't just stress, it was withdrawal. And I'd realize I didn't have the luxury of "just one" anymore. That option was gone. Whatever control I thought I had, I'd already handed it over a long time ago.

And slowly, beneath the chaos, little signs of healing began to show.

My sleep, though still rocky, started to deepen. I'd wake up feeling slightly more rested, a small but noticeable shift from the usual morning fog. The constant low-grade tremor in my hands, the one I'd chalked up to work stress, vanished. And then there was this new thing: moments of clarity. Just flashes, really. But enough to remember what it used to feel like to have a brain that worked cleanly.

By the end of week three, I was starting to find my footing, or at least building a few basic systems to keep me steady. Nothing elaborate. Just small, practical ways to stay ahead of temptation.

I started scheduling early morning meetings after events where I might normally have had a drink. The kind of logistical trick that made it harder to justify "just one" the night before. I stocked the fridge with non-alcoholic drinks that actually felt interesting: complex teas, zero-proof spirits, mocktails that weren't just juice with a straw. Having something in my hand during social stuff helped more than I'd expected.

I also got better at spotting my own triggers. Work stress, for sure. But also certain social environments, or even times of day. There was a window every afternoon around 5:30 when my brain would light up with that old, familiar script: "You've earned it. Just one." I learned to expect it, plan around it. Take a walk. Call Sarah. Make a fizzy drink with ice and lime and pretend for ten minutes that it was something stronger. Sometimes the illusion was enough to quiet the noise.

And then there was the group.

A few blocks from home, in a low-key community center in Park Slope, I found a secular recovery meeting that met once a week. No prayers. No Higher Power talk. Just people sharing stories, strategies, science, and, sometimes, silence. It wasn't dramatic. It wasn't anything I expected to work. But it helped.

Hearing other people talk about their spiral, how it started slowly, how the rules slipped, how the drink became a need instead of a want, it was like listening to my own story in someone else's voice. The details were different, but the arc was the same. That's what

HOWARD KANE

got me: the pattern. The predictability of it. I wasn't some outlier. I wasn't uniquely broken. I was just one more person caught in a very old, very familiar loop.

I didn't say much in those early meetings. I was still too cautious about privacy, about being seen, about what might happen if my name got attached to the word "recovery." But just being there, just listening, started to loosen something in me. The shame didn't feel quite as heavy when I saw how many others were carrying it too.

Sarah noticed.

"You seem... lighter after those meetings," she said one night.

I nodded. "They help. It's weird hearing someone else say the exact thing you've been thinking. Like, word for word. And they're not screw-ups. They're smart. They've built careers, families. They've just struggled with this, same as me."

She smiled, not smug, just steady. "That's why connection matters. Addiction isolates. Recovery doesn't."

It was one of many things she said in those early weeks that stuck with me. Sarah wasn't just my wife anymore. She'd quietly become my anchor. The one person who didn't flinch when I fell apart. Who didn't minimize what was happening, or try to fix it, but just walked beside me while I tried to figure it out.

Support without sugarcoating. Accountability without judgment.

That's what made all the difference.

On day thirty, I woke up before the alarm again. That was becoming normal. No groggy fumbling for the snooze button, no mental fog I had to shake off before remembering where I was or what day it was. I just woke up. Clear. Steady.

I lay there for a while, just checking in with myself. No thudding heart. No sour taste in my mouth. No crawling dread about what I might have said the night before, or how I'd shown up, or who I needed to apologize to. That low-level anxiety that had lived in my chest every morning, part hangover, part shame, part withdrawal, was gone. In its place was something quieter. Stillness, maybe. Or just space to breathe.

I wasn't under any illusion that thirty days meant I was cured. I'd heard enough in recovery meetings to know about the so-called "pink cloud," that early sobriety honeymoon when everything feels lighter, better, even euphoric, before the real work begins. I knew it wouldn't last forever.

But still, something real had shifted. My body had stopped rebelling. The shakes were gone. The cravings hadn't disappeared, but they had a rhythm now. I could anticipate them, outmaneuver them. Most of all, I'd made it through a full month of real life, meetings, dinners, weekend chaos with a kid, without leaning on alcohol to survive it.

I showered, shaved, got dressed like any other day. But it didn't feel like any other day. It felt like the beginning of something solid. Something earned.

Seven pounds lighter without trying. Clearer skin. Eyes less haunted. My thoughts sharper, my memory no longer Swiss cheese. And Alex. God, the way I could just be with him now. Not halfway there, not distracted, not vaguely hungover. Just there. Present.

Of course, it hadn't all been easy. I'd skipped parties I didn't trust myself to handle. I'd white-knuckled through dinners where the clinking of glasses made my skin crawl. I'd stared down old regrets I'd drowned for years and realized they were still waiting for me, exactly where I left them. But even with the discomfort, maybe because of it, I felt like I was getting closer to something true.

As I poured coffee in the kitchen, Sarah passed behind me, already dressed, her bag over her shoulder.

"Thirty days," she said, casual but not. A statement with weight.

"Thirty," I said back, and we both paused there for a beat.

"How do you feel?"

I thought about it. Really thought. "Like I'm starting to wake up," I said. "After being asleep for a long time."

She smiled, stepped closer, and straightened my tie. It was such a small, ordinary gesture, but it felt like everything. Like she saw me again. Not just the guy holding it together, but the one coming back to life.

THE DOUBLE LIFE OF A HIGH-FUNCTIONING ALCOHOLIC

"Welcome back," she said.

It wasn't a finish line. It wasn't even close. But it was a marker. A break from the years I spent orbiting alcohol like it was the sun and I was some loyal moon.

Thirty days sober.

A milestone I never thought I'd reach. And now, just the beginning of the real journey.

Chapter Seven

Quicksand: The First Slip

Y OU HEAR A LOT of neat, linear recovery stories. The fall. The decision. The tough early days. And then clarity. Momentum. A slow but steady climb out of the dark.

Mine didn't go like that.

Day 43 found me in a hotel bar in San Francisco, staring at a glass of eighteen-year-old Macallan. I had ordered it almost without thinking. The server placed it in front of me, and there it was glinting amber under the low lights, familiar and comforting like an old friend I hadn't seen in a while.

And just like that, six weeks of sobriety evaporated into rationalization.

I deserve this. It's one drink. It's been over a month. I'm fine.

The justifications came fast. Smooth. Polished. The same lines I'd used for years. The only difference now was that I could hear the lie in them, even as I reached for the glass.

I was in town for a major conference. My team had just nailed a huge presentation. We landed a big client we'd been chasing for over a year. It was a big win, the kind that usually ended with expensive liquor and loud laughter in a dark hotel bar. So when the client executive suggested a toast, my mouth said "yes" before my brain had a chance to weigh in.

And because I didn't want to just go along, I wanted to own it. I picked the priciest scotch on the menu. Like that made it more ceremonial. Like that somehow separated it from the guy I used to be.

I raised the glass. Smiled. Clinked.

The first sip hit like nostalgia. Smooth, warm, slightly sweet. A familiar fire curling down my throat and spreading through my chest. My body remembered. It welcomed the drink like a missing piece falling back into place.

And almost instantly, I felt the shame.

It came fast. Hot. Heavy. Like being caught in a lie you told too well.

Forty-three days of rebuilding trust, of healing, of waking up clear, undone by one impulsive moment I saw coming and still didn't stop.

I kept the conversation going, kept smiling, kept playing my role. But inside, it was chaos. One part of my brain was already plotting how to hide it, how to spin it when I got home, how to keep my sobriety count going like this night didn't happen. Another part just watched in disbelief at how fast it all collapsed.

And then, beneath all that, a darker voice. Calmer. Smoother.

See? You're fine. You're not like those people. You're in control.

Two hours later, I was three drinks in and floating in that soft buzz I used to call normal. I sat on the edge of the hotel bed, debating whether to call Sarah. I'd promised I would.

Instead, I texted: Exhausted from the presentation. Going to crash early. Great news though. We landed a big client! Will call in the morning. Love you.

It was disturbingly easy, slipping back into deception after weeks of trying to live honestly. As if that muscle memory had never really gone away.

I passed out fast, but at 3 a.m., I jolted awake. Heart racing. Mouth dry. That old familiar regret sitting heavy in my chest. My body didn't handle the alcohol like it used to. After weeks of healing, even a few drinks hit like a sledgehammer.

I stared at the ceiling, letting it sink in.

This wasn't just a slip. This was a crossroads.

I could come clean. Call Sarah. Go to a meeting as soon as I got back to New York. Start over, honestly. Or I could bury it. File it under "mistake," recommit in silence, pretend it hadn't happened.

Option two would protect my image. Keep everything neat and undisturbed. But it would also mean carrying this alone. Lying. Again.

By morning, I knew what I had to do.

Not because it was easy, but because it was the only way forward that didn't take me straight back into the quicksand I'd spent six weeks trying to climb out of.

"I drank last night," I said, no buildup, no small talk.

It was 6 a.m. in San Francisco. 9 a.m. in New York. Sarah picked up on the first ring.

She didn't respond right away. The silence stretched, just long enough for my stomach to tighten.

"I see," she said finally. Calm. Neutral. "How are you feeling about that?"

That caught me off guard. I expected disappointment. Maybe frustration. Not an open-ended question.

"Honestly? Ashamed. Surprised at how fast it happened. And... worried. Like, if I gave in that easily, what does that say about me?"

She let that hang for a second before answering. "That sounds like a pretty honest reaction."

So I told her everything. The win. The celebration. The automatic yes. How fast the old thinking came back. And how normal it all felt in the moment, until it didn't. Until the shame crept in before I'd even finished the first drink.

"It's textbook," I said. "I walked right into it. Put myself in a situation where not drinking felt awkward. Then made it worse by trying to act like it wasn't a big deal."

"And was it?" she asked. "Controllable, I mean."

I thought about that. "Sort of? I didn't spiral. I wasn't sloppy or reckless. But the fact that one drink so quickly became three? That part didn't feel intentional. It felt automatic. Like my brain had just been waiting for the green light."

She didn't say anything for a second. Then: "So what now?"

"I'm going to a meeting as soon as I get home. I'll tell them what happened. I'm going to reset the counter."

That last part hurt to say. Forty-three days. Gone in a few sips. But I knew it had to be done. Anything else would have been dishonest.

"That sounds like the right move," she said.

Then, quietly: "I'm proud of you for calling me. That's new."

That landed harder than I expected. She was right. In the past, I would have hidden it. Waited until the guilt got unbearable. Or until she noticed. Or until I slipped again and couldn't cover it up.

This time, I picked up the phone.

"I almost didn't," I said. "I almost talked myself into thinking it wasn't worth mentioning."

"But you didn't," she said. "You told me. That's what matters."

She was giving me something I hadn't considered, that the real test wasn't whether I stayed perfect. It was whether I stayed honest. And in that moment, that felt like progress. Not failure.

The meeting that night was held in the basement of a church in Park Slope. It wasn't dramatic or dimly lit or cinematic in any way. Just a circle of folding chairs under harsh fluorescent lights that made everything feel a little too honest, which was probably the point.

I had been going to this secular group for about six weeks. Until then, I mostly just listened. Took it in. Let the stories wash over me. But that night, I raised my hand.

"I'm Dave," I said, my voice catching a little more than I expected. "I'd been sober for forty-three days. Until two nights ago."

No gasps. No judgment. Just quiet, attentive faces. A few nods. People who'd been there.

"I was in San Francisco for work," I continued. "We landed a big client. It felt like a win. Someone suggested a toast, and I didn't plan not to drink, so I drank. Three scotches."

That last part sounded strange even to me. I didn't plan not to drink. It was the truth, and also the problem. I hadn't built the muscle for what to do in that exact kind of moment where alcohol was the default, where success meant celebration, and celebration meant drinking.

"I stayed professional," I said. "I didn't spiral. But the hardest part wasn't stopping after three drinks. The hardest part came after when I had to decide whether to be honest about it."

More nods. I wasn't telling a new story. I was telling a familiar one.

"There was a voice in my head saying, 'You don't need to reset your count. It was just one night. Doesn't mean anything.' But I knew if I did that, if I kept going like it hadn't happened, I'd be right back in the pattern that kept me stuck for years. So, I'm back at day two."

The room held a quiet for a second longer than usual. Then people started chiming in.

Michael, a lawyer who'd been sober for seven years, leaned forward slightly. "Relapse isn't outside the recovery story," he said. "It's part of it for a lot of us. What matters isn't that you slipped. It's that you came back. And you came back honest."

That hit me. Because it reframed the moment. It wasn't about failing at sobriety. It was about learning something I hadn't learned yet, how to stay grounded in situations that once felt automatic. The drinks weren't the issue. The blind spot was.

And now, I'd seen it.

That meeting didn't erase the shame. But it gave me a place to put it. It turned the night in San Francisco into a lesson, not a sentence. And for the first time, I realized: recovery isn't about never messing up.

It's about what you do the next morning. And the one after that.

The weeks after I slipped in San Francisco were different. Not dramatic, not chaotic, just sharper. Like someone had turned up the contrast on everything. I became aware, almost constantly, of how fragile early sobriety really was.

Before the slip, I had started to feel confident. Not cocky, exactly, but I was beginning to believe I had this under control. That I'd figured something out. Then three drinks reminded me how easily I could lose the thread.

The physical aftermath was what surprised me most. It wasn't a wild night. Just three drinks. But my body reacted like I'd poisoned it. The hangover was brutal. My heart raced, my sleep shattered. And the anxiety, it settled in like a fog that wouldn't lift for days. It was a different kind of sick. The kind that felt final. Like my body was done with alcohol. Not just tired of it. Done.

Oddly, that became useful. When cravings came, and they did, I didn't just think about what might happen emotionally or socially. I remembered the actual, physical fallout. That raw, chemical backlash. It made saying no feel less like willpower and more like self-defense.

Sarah picked up on the shift too. About two weeks after I got back, she said, "You seem different since San Francisco. More... vigilant?"

She was right. "I think I got cocky," I told her. "Six weeks in, I started thinking I had it figured out. And then I realized how fast it can fall apart."

"Is the vigilance bad?" she asked.

"Not bad," I said. "Just tiring. Every situation that used to be automatic, grabbing a drink to celebrate, having wine at dinner, unwinding after a long day, now requires a decision. It's like living in manual mode."

She nodded. "That's how trauma works," she said. "The brain goes on high alert, scanning for threats."

And that nailed it. Everything felt like a potential ambush. A toast. A client dinner. A casual Friday night. Each one asked for energy and focus I didn't always have.

"But it doesn't stay like that," she added. "Eventually, your brain builds new tracks. New defaults. It takes time, but it gets easier."

"How much time?" I asked. I'd asked her that same question in the early days, back when I couldn't sleep or think clearly and wondered if I ever would again.

"It depends," she said. "But a lot of people say around six months to a year, it starts to feel more natural."

That number, six months, felt far off. But not impossible. And something about hearing it framed this moment differently. I wasn't failing by finding sobriety exhausting. I was in a transition. I was doing what the brain does when it's learning something new: working hard, making mistakes, recalibrating.

I wasn't broken. I was building.

One unexpected result of slipping in San Francisco was that it forced me to stop hiding. At least a little.

Two of my team members, Raj and Elena, had been with me at the hotel bar. They'd seen me drink. They'd seen the hesitation. The weird energy. The tension I couldn't quite mask. And I knew the silence that followed would only feed speculation. So the day after we got back to New York, I asked them to grab coffee.

"I want to talk about what happened at the hotel bar," I said, right off the bat. No warm-up. Just straight in.

They exchanged a quick glance. It told me everything. I wasn't the only one thinking about it.

"I've been sober for about six weeks," I told them. "That night was a slip. It wasn't planned. And it's not something I want to pretend didn't happen."

Raj nodded slowly. "We kind of figured something was different," he said. "You've seemed clearer lately. Then when you ordered that scotch, it just didn't fit."

"We weren't sure if we should say anything," Elena added. "Didn't know if it was personal or none of our business."

That stopped me for a second. Because in my head, I'd always kept a hard line between my personal life and my role as a leader.

But clearly, my habits and my recent shift had been more visible than I'd realized.

"I'm not asking for anything," I said. "No special treatment. I just didn't want it to turn into some awkward thing everyone tiptoes around. I slipped, but I'm still committed to staying sober. That hasn't changed."

They both nodded, and Raj leaned in with something I didn't expect.

"Honestly? The team's noticed. Since you stopped drinking. You're more focused. More patient. There's been a shift in a good way."

That hit me harder than I expected. For years, I told myself my drinking never touched my work. That no one could tell. That I was sharp, reliable, dialed in. But if sobriety had brought noticeable improvements, what did that say about how I was showing up before?

"Thanks for telling me that," I said, and meant it. I didn't know what else to say.

Elena smiled. "We've got your back. Whatever you need."

And just like that, something shifted.

I had always thought revealing this part of myself at work would weaken me somehow. That it would chip away at my authority, my leadership. But instead, being honest, just a little bit, made things easier. It made the room feel less heavy. It made me feel less alone.

They still saw me as their boss. But maybe now, also as a person. And for the first time in a long time, that felt like a good thing.

Two months after slipping in San Francisco, I hit the forty-day mark again. It felt different this time. Less like something to celebrate, more like something to quietly acknowledge. Not triumphant, but honest. And maybe that was better.

I'd been through both parts now: the clean streak and the stumble. That contrast had reshaped how I viewed sobriety. It wasn't a streak I was chasing anymore. It was a practice. A process. Something to live in, not measure.

That night, while we were cleaning up after dinner, Sarah looked over at me and said, "Forty days. Again. How does it feel this time?"

I thought about it for a second before answering. "Less like I reached something, more like I'm building something. The first time, I treated it like a finish line. Now it feels more like a mile marker. There's a lot of road ahead."

She nodded, that small, knowing smile on her face. "So the slip wasn't wasted?"

"I wouldn't wish it on myself, but yeah," I said. "It forced me to stop fantasizing about what recovery should be and look at how it actually is for me."

"That's growth," she said. "Using it as feedback, not failure."

Before we could keep going, Alex came bounding into the kitchen. "Dad, can you help me with the solar system? I need to finish Saturn's rings."

"Yeah, buddy. Let's do it." I dried my hands and followed him to his room.

And as we sat on the floor, piecing together foam balls and fishing wire, I noticed how different this moment was from what it used to be. In the past, I would have already had two or three drinks by now. Maybe more. I would have helped with the project, sure, but only in body. My mind would have been foggy, my patience thin, my attention drifting toward the next refill.

Tonight, I was clear. I was in it. I wasn't rushing to get back to the couch or hiding behind a drink. I was just there with my son, building Saturn.

That, more than any number, felt like progress.

The slip in San Francisco had felt like sinking, like the ground had disappeared beneath me. But I hadn't gone under. I'd caught myself. Reached for help. Climbed out with a better map. That night reminded me that recovery isn't a straight shot. There are wrong turns, setbacks, recalculations. But it's still a path, not a pit.

And as Alex beamed while showing me how he'd engineered the rings with clear thread and glitter glue, I felt nothing but gratitude for this quiet, sober evening, and for the chance to get it right the second time around.

Because this was what it was about. Not just not drinking, but being here for the parts that mattered. One decision, one evening, one ordinary, beautiful moment at a time.

Chapter Eight

The Survival Guide: Building a Sober Toolkit

F IVE MONTHS INTO SOBRIETY, this time uninterrupted since my slip in San Francisco, I found myself gripping the railing on the rooftop of a sleek Manhattan hotel, trying to steady myself against a craving that felt like it might lift me off the ground.

Inside, just behind the glass doors, my team was celebrating our biggest client win of the year. Champagne flutes, laughter, the soft buzz of pride and alcohol. It was all playing out just the way it used to. But this time, I was not part of it.

I had ducked out five minutes earlier under the excuse of making a quick call, but in truth, I needed air. I needed space from the sound of champagne corks and the rising volume of voices. Those sensory triggers still had the power to rattle me, even after months without a drink.

The craving hit hard. Not just a passing thought, but a full-body desire, like my brain had flipped into another mode and was demanding, now. It didn't matter that I knew better. Cravings don't negotiate with reason.

I pulled out my phone and texted Michael, my recovery buddy, the corporate lawyer from my support group.

At work celebration. Everyone is drinking. Craving is strong. Need backup.

His reply came fast, like he had been expecting it:

Remember your why. What's the story you want to write tonight?

That was a line we used often in our meetings. The idea was simple. Play it forward. Don't just think about the drink. Think about what comes after the drink.

So I stood there, the city buzzing beneath me, and ran the two stories in my head.

First scenario: I go back inside, take the champagne when it's offered. The craving eases. I feel included, maybe even a little proud of myself for "just one." But then one turns into three because that's what it always does. I wake up tomorrow with a pounding head, guilt in my gut, and five months of hard-won sobriety wiped away. I have to tell Sarah. I have to tell the group. I start from zero.

Second scenario: I go back in, say no thanks, stick to my sparkling water. The craving sticks around for a bit, then fades because that's what it always does too. I wake up with a clear head, five months still intact, and a little more confidence in my ability to handle whatever comes next.

That made it simple. Not easy, but simple.

I texted Michael:

Thanks. Staying the course. Will check in later.

Then I took three slow breaths. The kind of breathing they taught me early on, to give my brain a beat to catch up before acting. I straightened my jacket and walked back inside.

And just like that, the moment passed.

This, I realized, was what real recovery looked like five months in. Not the disappearance of cravings, but the arrival of tools to deal with them. Not pretending discomfort doesn't exist, but learning how to sit with it, move through it, and stay standing.

I didn't feel heroic. I didn't even feel particularly strong. But I did feel steady. And for someone who used to chase relief in every glass, that was more than enough.

Four months ago, I might have caved. Three months ago, I might have skipped the event entirely. But now I was learning how to stay in the room with my team, with my values, with myself.

That rooftop moment was not perfection. It was progress. And for once, that was exactly what I needed.

At first, the idea of a sober toolkit felt too simplistic. Like all I needed was the right set of tools and I could patch up a lifetime problem the way you fix a leaky faucet with a wrench. But addiction, at least mine, was not mechanical. It was emotional, neurological, deeply human. It didn't respond to tools the way a loose bolt does.

But over time, I began to see the value in having real, practical strategies. Not as miracle fixes, but as something more reliable than willpower alone. These were not magic bullets. They were small, learned responses, muscle memory for the brain, that gave me something to reach for when the urge to drink came knocking.

By the time I hit five months of sobriety, that toolkit had become second nature. It didn't feel like effort anymore. It felt like preparation.

There was a night on a Manhattan rooftop when the urge to drink crashed in hard. Laughter and champagne flutes surrounded me, and my skin prickled with anxiety. For a moment, the old instinct wanted to say yes and reach for a glass. Instead, I pressed my hand against the cool metal railing, closed my eyes, and counted to ten. That small pause gave my brain just enough time to remember why I was here in the first place. By the time I walked back inside, the craving had started to pass.

A week later, at a client dinner, I watched the waiter circle with a bottle of pinot. The familiar script ran through my mind. Just have one, celebrate, nobody will notice. I let myself imagine the whole evening, playing it out in my mind. If I took that drink, how would I feel in the morning? If I didn't, what would tomorrow look like? It was never about the first sip. It was always about the regret or the relief that followed. That night, I chose to stick with sparkling water and woke up the next day with a clear head, grateful for the decision I made.

At crowded gatherings, anxiety buzzed in my chest and the urge to self-medicate showed up fast. Instead of pouring a drink, I would slip outside for a few deep breaths or call Michael, my recovery buddy. We would talk for five minutes, just enough to reset. Those little swaps never felt dramatic, but they helped me get through the moment without falling back into the old routine.

Sometimes people would nudge me to join in. "Come on, just one," or, "Are you on some kind of cleanse?" I got better at handling these moments. I'd smile and say, "Just feeling better without it lately," or, "On a bit of a health kick." Short and simple, never defensive. The less I explained, the easier it got.

For every big event, I made sure I had an exit strategy. If the room started to feel heavy or temptation built up, I always had my own ride, a reason to leave, or someone ready to cover for me. Just knowing I could step away if I needed to make it easier to stay.

I kept in touch with Sarah or Michael, sometimes by just firing off a text from the bathroom or the street. "All good here." Other times, if I was really struggling, it was just, "Tell me I don't need this." Their replies were like lifelines.

And the mornings were their own kind of reward. I would wake up, notice the quiet in my mind and the absence of shame, and just breathe it in for a moment. Those small victories, stacked day after day, started to build a new kind of confidence. I was learning that it didn't require a checklist, just a bit of intention and a willingness to show up for my own life.

These things were not theoretical anymore. I had used them, adjusted them, relied on them. Some nights, they were the only thing between me and a drink. But with practice, they became less like emergency measures and more like instincts.

What mattered most wasn't the tools themselves. It was what they represented. That I was treating sobriety as something active, not passive. I wasn't just not drinking. I was showing up for this every day. Practicing it. Getting better at it.

And like any skill, the more I used it, the more it felt like mine.

"You talk about sobriety differently now," Sarah said as we strolled through a park one evening. Alex was running ahead, chasing some invisible treasure along the path. "It used to be all about what you were giving up. Now it sounds like it's about what you're building."

She caught me off guard, not because she was wrong, but because I hadn't realized it myself. "Yeah," I said after a beat. "I guess it has changed. At first, it felt like I was losing something. Now it feels more like I'm gaining something new."

She smiled. "It's like watching someone learn a new language. At first, it's all flashcards and rules. You're constantly translating in your head. But eventually, you start thinking in that language."

That hit home. In early sobriety, everything felt like translation. I was rewriting every familiar situation, like dinners, celebrations, and Friday nights, into some clunky, alcohol-free version of itself. But now, five months in, I was starting to just live those moments as they were. No conversion required.

"The brain is amazing that way," Sarah said, slipping into doctor mode, which I had grown to find oddly comforting. "Every time you choose not to drink, you are reinforcing new neural pathways. And the old ones, those default drink-at-this-moment ones, they weaken. That's how change happens."

I nodded. That idea of neuroplasticity had been one of the most helpful ways for me to think about recovery. This wasn't about willpower or character. I wasn't battling some broken part of me. I was rewiring a brain that had been trained over decades to turn to alcohol in certain situations.

"It's still hard sometimes," I admitted. "There are moments where the old wiring just lights up. Like a reflex."

"That's totally normal," she said. "Those old paths don't vanish completely. They just get quieter with time. Less automatic."

We walked for a bit in silence, and I thought about how much that understanding had helped me. Cravings used to feel like personal failures, proof I hadn't changed. Now I saw them for what they were: echoes of the past, habits trying to hold on. Not good or bad. Just signals. They didn't mean I was broken. They meant I was healing.

"Dad, look at this!" Alex's voice cut through my thoughts. He was crouched by the path, pointing into the grass.

We caught up to him and saw what he had found. A small box turtle was slowly making its way across the trail. We all kneeled down, watching in quiet fascination. Alex was beaming, eyes wide, as if he had discovered buried treasure. And in a way, he had.

A year ago, I might have missed that moment. I would have been distracted, hungover, or already thinking about the next drink. But now, I was right there, completely present. I was watching that turtle with my son, not just as a dad checking the box on some parental duty, but as someone who was truly there.

That, I realized, was the most surprising gift of sobriety. It wasn't just about feeling better in the morning or having a clearer head at work. It was this. I could experience life without a filter. I was fully awake and fully available. I was not numbed. I was not half-there.

As we continued walking, I understood something else. The real shift, the one that mattered most, wasn't in how I felt or what I drank or didn't drink. It was in how I saw sobriety itself. It wasn't a loss anymore. It wasn't something to endure. It was something I was building. It was something I got to explore.

It wasn't a restriction. It was an expansion.

Not everyone understood or appreciated the shift I was going through. Six months into sobriety, I was still getting nudged, sometimes gently, sometimes not so much, by people who had known me during my drinking years. Especially in work settings, the idea that I no longer drank was still surprising to some and quietly threatening to others.

"Come on, one drink isn't going to kill you," said Jim Barton, a longtime client, as we wrapped up a quarterly review over lunch. "We always grab a whiskey after these meetings. It's tradition."

Jim and I had been working together for over five years. Yes, we had shared plenty of post-meeting drinks. This was his way of celebrating a job well done, and he clearly expected me to fall in line, just like always.

"I appreciate the offer," I said, sliding into the response I had practiced. "But I'm not drinking these days. Just a health thing that's been working well for me."

He looked at me for a second, eyebrows knitting just slightly. "Is it forever? Or just a cleanse thing?"

That question came up a lot. Most people didn't ask because they genuinely cared. It was more about figuring out how uncom-

fortable my decision should make them. If it was just a temporary health kick, they could shrug it off. If it was permanent,
that was a different story. It was a bigger mirror.

"It's indefinite," I said. "Honestly, I've been feeling so much
better. I don't see a reason to go back."

Jim paused. "Better how?"

I debated how far to go. Jim wasn't a close friend. He was
a client, and our relationship had always lived in that space
where business and drinks blurred the line. Still, I didn't want
to dodge completely.

"Sleep, energy, mental clarity," I said. "And I was leaning
on alcohol to deal with stress in ways that weren't helping
anymore."

He leaned back and let out a breath, almost like a confession.
"Yeah. My doctor keeps telling me to cut back. Says my liver
numbers aren't great. And this." He patted his stomach. "Isn't
exactly going over well at home."

And just like that, the vibe shifted. We were not negotiating
whether I would join him for a drink. We were two guys in our
forties talking about how booze had started taking more than
it gave.

"How about coffee?" I offered. "There's a great spot around
the corner."

Jim smiled. "Sure. But you're still picking up the tab. Some
traditions are sacred."

It was a small moment, but one that mattered. This wasn't just about resisting pressure. It was about keeping relationships intact by shifting them slightly, changing the environment, changing the rhythm, but not walking away. The old version of me might have declined the drink but also the moment, retreating instead of finding a new way to connect.

Not every interaction went this smoothly. Some people took my sobriety personally, like I was silently judging them. Others didn't know how to act around me without a drink in their hand. And yes, a few relationships just faded out. Those were the ones that were built on alcohol more than anything else.

But more often than not, being honest without being dramatic, and open without being evangelical, seemed to work. It let the people who mattered know I was still here, just showing up a little differently. And that, in its own quiet way, helped keep me steady too.

One of the most unexpected and useful tools in my sobriety toolkit came from Aiden, a junior data scientist on my team. I didn't even know he was in recovery until after my slip in San Francisco. But once I started being more open about my own sobriety, it created a space for others to open up too.

We were supposed to be talking about project timelines during a one-on-one, but somehow the conversation drifted. Aiden shared that he'd been sober for three years after a rough stretch in college. I asked him what had helped most in the early days, and without hesitation, he said, "Changing how I thought about urges."

At first, I didn't follow. He went on, "I used to think cravings meant I was failing. Like, if I wanted to drink, it meant I was doing something wrong or that I was weak."

I nodded. I'd felt the same. That heavy feeling of shame, even if I didn't act on the craving.

"Then my counselor said something that stuck," Aiden continued. "He told me to think of urges as data, not directives."

That caught my attention.

"What do you mean?" I asked.

"Well, we're data people," he said. "We read patterns, signals, anomalies. What if a craving isn't an order, like 'go drink now,' but just a data point? Something that tells you your system is under pressure? You don't have to act on it, just read it. Understand it."

That hit hard. He'd put into words what I hadn't yet figured out on my own. As a data scientist, I was wired to analyze, not to panic at every blip on the dashboard. So why not apply that same thinking to recovery?

When I felt the pull to drink, I started pausing and asking: What's going on here? Am I tired? Stressed? Feeling insecure? Lonely? What was this craving trying to tell me? Usually, it wasn't about alcohol. It was about something underneath, something I could actually address if I paid attention.

Instead of treating urges like failures, I began seeing them as signals. If I was anxious, I'd step outside and breathe. If I was lonely, I'd text a friend. If I was just bored or stuck in a routine that used to involve alcohol, I'd switch things up. Aiden helped me realize that the craving itself wasn't the enemy. It was the response that mattered.

He also gave me another idea I ran with: tracking. "I kept a log," he said. "Like we do for model behavior. Craving intensity, what triggered it, what I did, and how it turned out. Over time, you start seeing patterns. You get proof you're making progress, even if it doesn't feel like it that day."

That night, I built a simple spreadsheet to do just that. Nothing fancy. Just a record of the cravings, the triggers, what tools I used, and whether they helped. It gave me a sense of control, a way to turn something vague and emotional into something I could measure and learn from.

It worked. On the bad days, when I felt stuck or discouraged, I could look at that log and see that things were, in fact, getting better. The cravings weren't as strong. I was responding faster, more effectively. The data didn't lie.

Recovery hadn't changed who I was. It had just shifted how I used my skills. Instead of analyzing datasets for clients, I was analyzing the signals inside myself. And that shift from reacting emotionally to responding with curiosity made all the difference.

By six months, the way I thought about sobriety had changed. In the beginning, it was all about survival, just getting through the cravings, dodging temptation, and trying not to screw up. My toolkit was basically a first-aid kit. Now, it had started to feel more like a full-on lifestyle guide.

I wasn't just reacting anymore. I was building a life where alcohol didn't have a seat at the table. The tools I'd collected weren't just about saying no to a drink. They helped me understand why I'd wanted to drink in the first place, and how to handle those same situations differently.

I realized how far I'd come during a bedtime conversation with Alex. He was eight by then, and in that way kids have, he saw things clearly.

"Dad," he said as I tucked him in, "are you still doing that thing where you don't drink the grown-up drinks?"

"Yeah," I said, caught a little off guard. "Why do you ask?"

He shrugged. "You and Mom used to talk about it a lot when you thought I wasn't listening. Now you don't."

And he was right. At first, Sarah and I were always talking about it, checking in, troubleshooting, managing the whole thing like a fragile situation. But over time, those conversations had faded, not because sobriety stopped mattering, but because it stopped feeling like a crisis. It had just become life.

"It's gotten easier," I told him. "Kind of like when you learned to ride your bike. At first, you had to think about every little thing. Now you just get on and ride."

He nodded, and then said something that floored me.

"Good. You're more fun now, anyway."

"More fun?" I asked, half-laughing.

"Yeah. You play with me more. You don't fall asleep on the couch all the time. And you remember stuff."

There it was. Simple, honest, and absolutely right. For Alex, the change wasn't about what I didn't do. It was about what I did do. I was around. I was awake. I kept my promises.

As I turned off his light and closed the door, I thought about how different my life had become. Not because I'd become an expert at resisting temptation, but because I'd become better at actually living, being present, enjoying the small things, and showing up for my family.

That's what recovery started to look like at six months. Not a daily fight, but a growing sense of normal. A version of life where alcohol wasn't just avoided. It was irrelevant. It had less and less to offer.

The tools that once helped me survive were now helping me thrive. Not by forcing me to give something up, but by showing me what I'd been missing. More focus. More fun. More love. More life.

And maybe that's the real point of a sober toolkit. Not just staying sober, but building a life so full, so honest, and so present that you don't want to escape it anymore.

You've reached the midpoint of *The Double Life of a High-Functioning Alcoholic*

Thank you for coming this far with me. There are still plenty of twists, honest moments, and stories left in the rest of the book, and I hope you'll stick around for the journey ahead.

Before you dive back in, I just wanted to pause for a moment and ask: if you're finding the book meaningful so far, would you consider leaving a quick, honest review on Amazon? Even a few sentences can help new readers find the story and makes a big difference for indie authors like me.

Thank you for reading and now, on to the rest of the story!

Chapter Nine

The Turbulent Waters

NINE MONTHS INTO SOBRIETY, I found myself wide awake at 3 AM, staring at the ceiling while Sarah slept beside me. I wasn't restless in the old sense. No guilt hangover. No replaying the night before. But something deeper had shifted. There was a strange buzz beneath the surface, like my emotions were trying to tell me something and I couldn't quite hear it.

I thought sobriety was supposed to bring peace. After nine months, shouldn't I be leveling out? Instead, I felt like I was unraveling emotionally just as everything else, my health, my routine, my family life, was finally coming together.

No one really warned me about, at least not in a way I could hear, was how emotional sobriety would be. I don't mean the deep, dramatic soul-searching kind of emotional. I mean the everyday feelings that started hitting me like unexpected weather: anxiety, sadness, random bursts of joy, even awe. Everything felt dialed up.

Without alcohol to dull the edges, the world got louder and brighter. Sometimes it was beautiful. Sometimes it was overwhelming.

There was this moment when I was watching a documentary about space with Alex. We were on the couch, half-snuggled under a blanket, and it was just one of those low-key, nothing-special nights. Until I found myself crying.

Not sobbing. Just tears, quietly rolling down my face while astronauts floated through the silence of space and Carl Sagan talked about stardust.

Alex looked up. "Dad, are you crying?"

I laughed a little. "I guess I am."

"But it's not sad," he said, genuinely puzzled. "It's just about stars and stuff."

"Sometimes people cry when something's beautiful," I told him. "Not just when they're sad."

He thought about that. "Like how Mom cried at my piano recital even though I didn't mess up?"

"Exactly like that."

He nodded, satisfied with that answer, then leaned back into me and rested his head on my shoulder. And in that moment, with the weight of him pressed gently against me and the vastness of the universe glowing on the screen in front of us, I felt something I hadn't felt in a long time: full, unfiltered presence.

It hit me hard, how many of these little moments I'd missed or dulled over the years. How many times I'd been there but not really there.

I brought it up at my weekly recovery meeting. "I feel like I'm backsliding," I said. "Physically I feel great. But emotionally? I'm all over the place."

People in the circle nodded. One of the members, a clinical psychologist, explained that this was actually common. After the body adjusts to life without alcohol, the brain takes much longer to catch up. Emotions that had been numbed for years don't just return. They come back in waves, sometimes harder and more intense than you expect. And it can happen months, even a year, into sobriety.

She said something that stuck with me: "You're not going backward. You're feeling things fully, maybe for the first time in decades."

It was a turning point. I started looking at these emotional flare-ups not as setbacks, but as signs that I was healing. I wasn't broken. I was re-learning how to feel without a chemical buffer. I realized I needed to take extra care of myself during this phase:

get enough sleep, stay active, eat well, and most importantly, stay connected to people who understood.

That night, when I found myself awake again, I didn't fight it. I just lay there and paid attention, like a scientist observing data. What had set me off that day? What was I feeling right now? The emotions didn't vanish, but they lost some of their power. They weren't a verdict on how I was doing. They were just part of the process.

And that changed everything.

Nine months in, I found myself staring at the kitchen window one morning, coffee gone cold in my hands. The world outside looked gray and jittery.

I finally said it out loud to Sarah after Alex left for school. "I don't get it. I'm doing all the right things, meetings, sleep, exercise, but lately it feels like my emotions are all over the place. It's almost like I'm starting from scratch. Like I'm raw."

Sarah listened, quiet, stirring her coffee. She didn't launch into science or therapy talk. She just let the silence stretch.

"Does it get easier?" I finally asked.

She reached across the table and squeezed my hand. "You're showing up. That's the hard part," she said. "Maybe this is what healing feels like."

I let her words hang there. I wanted advice, a fix, some three-step program to rebuild myself, but all she offered was presence. In that quiet, I realized I wasn't being asked to solve anything. I was being asked to feel it. To stay.

"Do you think I should talk to someone?" I asked. "Like a therapist who knows this territory?"

Sarah reached across the table and took my hand. "I think that would be a great step. Not because you're doing something wrong, but because it could make this part easier. You've handled the behavior change. Now you're ready for the deeper work."

That made sense to me. This wasn't about fixing something broken. It was about growing into the next phase of who I was becoming, someone who didn't just avoid the bottle but could face life head-on, feelings and all.

Later that day, walking to the train, I caught my reflection in a dark shop window and barely recognized the man looking back. Tired, yes, but alive in a way I hadn't felt before. It was a feeling like someone learning to walk after a long time sitting still. The world felt sharp around the edges, unpredictable and uncomfortable. But underneath all that, I felt something close to hope. I was building something new, even if I didn't yet know what to call it.

The first few months in therapy with Dr. Russell were nothing like I expected. I came in ready for a list of strategies, a plan to fix whatever felt so raw inside me. Instead, most sessions felt like wading through fog. I'd sit across from him, listing the ways my life looked good on paper but felt upside down inside.

One afternoon, after talking in circles about how easily I got overwhelmed these days, I finally blurted it out. "I just don't understand why I feel everything so much more now. Before, things barely made a dent. Now I cry at car commercials, or get set off by a bad email at work. It's like being a teenager again, only with bills and gray hair."

Dr. Russell just listened. He let the room stay quiet, like he was giving my confusion space to breathe. Then he asked, "What do you usually do with all that feeling?"

I shrugged. "I try to push it down. Sometimes I get irritable. Or I just want to check out. Old habit, I guess."

He nodded, nothing more. No lecture. No big medical explanation. Just curiosity. I found myself looking at the carpet, searching for words. "Back when I was drinking, I could turn this off. That's probably the whole reason I kept going as long as I did. Now it's like there's no buffer."

He just said, "What's that like?"

I laughed, not because it was funny, but because it was true. "It's exhausting. Everything is louder. Sometimes it feels like I missed the years when people figured out how to handle this stuff."

We sat for a while longer. He never gave me the speech about how alcohol numbs feelings or stunts growth. He just kept asking questions, nudging me to notice what was happening. Week by week, I saw the pattern. The more I stayed with those hard feelings, the less scary they became. Some days I still flinched. But every once in a while, I realized I was handling things differently. I didn't explode over a bad day at work. I apologized to Sarah without trying to win the argument. I let myself feel sad and didn't immediately reach for a distraction.

It hit me, slowly, that maybe this was the work. Maybe I was catching up on something I skipped. It wasn't comfortable, but it started to feel possible. I was learning how to feel things I used to run from, and with time, I wasn't running anymore.

Navigating leadership without the crutch of alcohol was like learning to ride a bike all over again, except this time the training wheels were gone and the road was full of unexpected turns.

Leading a team of twenty data scientists across different time zones had always been a juggling act. But in the past, I had a secret weapon. A glass of scotch at the end of a long day was my way of unwinding after a tough client call, marking the end of a stressful project, or smoothing over the discomfort of workplace conflicts. Without that, I had to face the full weight of these challenges head-on.

One particular incident stands out. A senior team member was consistently missing deadlines on a high-stakes project. In my drinking days, I might have avoided the confrontation, choosing instead to vent over drinks with colleagues. But now, I had to address the issue directly, without any liquid courage.

Drawing from techniques I had learned in therapy, I prepared not just the talking points but also braced myself emotionally. I identified my own triggers around conflict and planned how to respond calmly, no matter how the conversation unfolded. The meeting was uncomfortable, but it led to a constructive plan that addressed the performance issues while offering support. It was a more effective outcome than any I had achieved through avoidance or criticism in the past.

Sobriety was reshaping my leadership style. I was becoming more present, more emotionally attuned, and better equipped to handle the complexities of interpersonal dynamics. This transformation didn't go unnoticed. Raj remarked during a check-in, "You're more consistent now. Before, we never knew which version of you we'd get. Now, there's a steadiness, even when things are stressful."

His words highlighted a crucial point. While I might have felt more emotionally volatile internally, externally I was more consistent. Without the highs and lows induced by alcohol, my team experienced a leader who was steady and reliable.

This journey reinforced what my therapist had suggested: that emotional growth in recovery is not separate from professional development, it is integral to it. By learning to regulate my emotions without alcohol, I wasn't just becoming a healthier individual. I was evolving into a more effective leader.

The stretch between day 100 and day 300 of sobriety was unexpectedly tough. Honestly, it hit harder than the first hundred days. Early on, there is a kind of urgency. Your body is detoxing, you are white-knuckling your way through cravings, and you are constantly reminded of how bad things were. Every clear-headed morning feels like a little victory.

But somewhere after that hundred-day mark, things changed. The crisis had passed. The physical stuff had mostly sorted itself out. There wasn't the daily drama of early recovery to keep me focused. That is when the real grind began, the part where staying sober felt less like escaping disaster and more like choosing a different kind of life every single day, with no finish line in sight.

At one meeting, I vented about how I was feeling: disconnected, restless, and weirdly low even though things were technically going fine. Michael, a guy in our group who had a few years under his belt, said, "Think of it like running a marathon. The first few miles are adrenaline. The last stretch, you can see the finish line. But the middle miles? That's where the real work happens. That's where you find out why you're running."

That landed. This middle stretch of sobriety was not some personal failure. It was just the part where the excitement fades and the habits either deepen or unravel. I was not falling apart. I was just in the hard part.

There were not any big turning points during this phase. What got me through were the tiny, boring victories. Waking up without a hangover. Handling a stressful email without needing a drink to "take the edge off." Showing up to a birthday party, drinking club soda, and still having fun. These moments stacked up like bricks, slowly building a life that felt solid. Not dramatic. Just steady.

Something else shifted too. I stopped thinking of myself as "Dave who doesn't drink." That label felt temporary, like I was just holding my breath. But around this time, it started to fade. I was not the guy resisting temptation anymore. I was just Dave. Someone who shows up, deals with life, and does not need alcohol to do it.

I noticed this shift one evening when Alex asked for help with a science project. He had to build a model of the respiratory system, something with balloons and straws and a rubber sheet acting like a diaphragm. It was fiddly, detailed work. In the old days, I might have helped for twenty minutes before pouring myself a drink and calling it a night.

But this time, I sat with him at the kitchen table, fully engaged. We laughed as we tested the model. When the balloons inflated, Alex lit up. "Dad, this is awesome! We make a good team."

"We do," I said, and I meant it. That moment hit me harder than any milestone chip or congratulatory text. Not because of what I had stopped doing but because of what I was finally able to do.

Later, after he went to bed, I found myself tweaking the model, making sure it would work perfectly for his class. I did not even notice the time passing. Sarah walked in and raised an eyebrow. "You've been at that for three hours," she said.

"Really?" I looked at the clock. "Didn't feel like it."

She smiled. "That's the difference I see in you. Before, you might have bailed after twenty minutes or disappeared into a drink. Now, you're here for the whole thing."

She was right. That is what this stretch of recovery was about. It was not just not drinking. It was learning how to stay through boredom, stress, discomfort, even joy without needing an escape hatch.

This middle period was not easy. But it gave me something early sobriety could not: a deeper understanding of what I was building. I was not just removing alcohol. I was rediscovering presence. And as it turned out, that presence with my son, my wife, my team, and myself was worth every uncomfortable mile.

Around ten months in, something started to change. Not in a dramatic, life-altering way, but like the slow turning of a dimmer switch. The emotional chaos that had marked the past few months was still there, but it was not as erratic. The highs and lows were still intense, but they stopped ambushing me in the middle of normal days.

Dr. Russell called this phase "emotional differentiation." It is a clinical term, but what it really meant was that I was finally starting to put names to my feelings. Instead of everything swirling together in a big storm cloud labeled "bad," I could start picking out what was actually going on: disappointment, frustration, insecurity, and grief. Each emotion had its own shape now, its own texture. And because of that, they were easier to handle.

"It's like expanding your emotional vocabulary," he explained one day. "You're moving from feeling overwhelmed to actually understanding what's happening inside."

That clicked for me. It was the difference between feeling like a failure after a tough meeting versus realizing, "No, this is just disappointment because something I cared about didn't land the way I hoped." Once I could label the feeling, I could actually deal with it. Maybe adjust the plan, talk it out with someone, or even just sit with it for a bit without spiraling.

I was not trying to get rid of the intensity anymore. I was learning how to use it, like feedback instead of a fire alarm. Emotions were not enemies to fight off or run from. They were information. They were signals that something mattered, that I was invested, that I cared.

This shift made a big difference in how I thought about my recovery too. Earlier on, I would fall into this trap where any bad day meant I was doing sobriety "wrong." If I felt low or insecure or anxious, I would assume I was sliding backward. I saw things in black and white. Either I was killing it or I was failing.

Now, with a bit more emotional clarity, I saw it differently. Sobriety was not about staying in some eternal good mood. It was about facing life head-on, good, bad, and messy, and staying sober through all of it. Feeling sad did not mean I was failing. It meant I was human. It meant I was not checking out.

That realization softened things. I stopped grading myself on every emotional fluctuation. Instead of asking, "Am I doing recovery right today?" I started asking, "Am I showing up?" If the answer was yes, even on a rough day, that was enough.

And over time, that gentler mindset became part of my rhythm. I did not have to control how I felt every second. I just had to keep making the same choice not to drink, no matter what was going on inside. The rest, I trusted, would continue to settle with time.

As I got closer to my one-year mark without alcohol, I started looking back and what struck me most was not just how far I had come, but how differently the journey had unfolded from what I expected.

In the beginning, I figured the hardest part would be the first few weeks. That was when the cravings were sharp, the routines were deeply ingrained, and my body still expected its regular dose of alcohol. I braced myself for that part. And yes, those early days were tough. But they were also clear-cut and black-and-white in a way that made decisions easier, even if the discomfort was real.

What I had not anticipated was how the stretch between 100 and 300 days, those so-called "middle miles," would turn out to be the real test. Not because the cravings came back stronger, but because everything got more subtle and more complex. The drama of withdrawal was gone, replaced by the quiet, steady grind of showing up for life every day without the artificial boosts I once relied on.

During that time, I had to build entirely new skills I did not even know I lacked. How to regulate my emotions without shutting them down. How to navigate social situations where drinking was the default, without making it weird or turning into a walking PSA. How to lead at work without the evening drink to smooth the stress. And, maybe hardest of all, how to live without constantly ducking behind a drink when things felt uncomfortable or raw.

There were days when I felt on edge for no clear reason. Nights when sleep just would not come, no matter how exhausted I was. Moments when I missed that warm rush of alcohol not because I wanted to spiral again, but because I missed how easy it made everything feel. I stood in rooms full of people laughing and sipping cocktails and felt like I was floating just outside the frame.

But here is the thing: those were the moments that moved me forward the most.

That emotional turbulence, the irritability, the awkwardness, the quiet discomfort, was not a setback. It was the work. It was what forced me to grow. Without alcohol blurring the edges, I had to actually connect, actually lead, actually feel. I had to find real confidence, not the kind that came from a drink, but the kind that came from doing hard things over and over and realizing I could.

Now, a year in, I do not just feel grateful that I stopped drinking. I feel grateful for the whole messy, challenging stretch that came after, especially those middle months. They were rough, but they stripped away old habits and beliefs I did not even realize I was clinging to. They reshaped how I relate to myself, to other people, to the world.

This one-year milestone does not feel like a finish line. It feels like a solid place to stop, take a breath, and look around before moving forward again. There will be more challenges and more surprises, but I am walking into the next phase with tools I did not have a year ago and a steadier hand on the wheel.

The middle miles were not easy, but they were essential. They did not pull me off course. They were the course. And because of them, I am not just sober. I am more honest, more grounded, and more ready for what comes next.

Chapter Ten

The Challenge of Normalcy: Years One to Three

T HE MORNING OF MY one-year sobriety anniversary slipped in quietly, almost unnoticed. Just a regular Saturday in April. I was up before my alarm and went through my now-familiar routine. Some meditation, a workout, then coffee. Same as most mornings.

Sarah wandered into the kitchen, still in pajamas, and gave me a kiss on the temple.

"Happy anniversary," she said as she reached for her mug.

"You remembered," I said, genuinely surprised. We hadn't talked about making a big deal of it.

"Of course I remembered. Three hundred and sixty-five days? That's huge." She sat across from me. "So... how does it feel?"

I thought about it. "Honestly? Quieter than I imagined. When I first quit, making it a year felt like this massive mountain. I thought I'd feel different somehow. Transformed. But it's just a Saturday."

Sarah smiled. "That might be the best part. Sobriety has become so normal it doesn't feel like a big event anymore."

She was right. That was the real victory. Not some grand moment of fireworks, but the way sobriety had slowly woven itself into the fabric of everyday life. Not drinking wasn't a huge decision I had to make every morning anymore. It had just become who I was.

Later, I got a text from Michael, my recovery buddy: 365 days. Proud of you, man. Remember when you couldn't even imagine a sober weekend?

I laughed. I remembered all too well. Back then, even a few hours felt impossible. And now? It had become background noise. Quiet, steady, constant.

That evening, Sarah and Alex surprised me with a little celebration. Just us, no speeches, no fuss. Alex helped bake a lopsided cake with "1 year" scrawled in blue icing. It was perfect.

While we were eating, Alex looked at me seriously. "So you haven't had any grown-up drinks for a whole year?"

"That's right," I said.

"Are you never going to have them again? Like... ever?"

It was such a kid question. Simple, honest, looking for a clear answer. Adults usually dance around that kind of thing. Maybe someday, or we'll see. But kids want the lines drawn.

"That's the plan," I told him. "I feel better without them."

He nodded. "Cake's better anyway," he said, chocolate frosting smeared at the corner of his mouth.

We all laughed, and in that moment I felt something unexpected: freedom. Not the dramatic kind I used to fantasize about, but a quiet release from the grip alcohol once had on my life, from the way it had shaped how I saw myself.

One year sober. Not an ending, not some perfect transformation. Just a life, steady and recalibrated. One where ordinary Saturdays are more than enough.

The second year of sobriety caught me off guard. I thought the hard part was behind me. The early days had been about survival, getting through each hour, sometimes each minute, without picking up a drink. But now, with the physical cravings mostly gone and my daily routine stable, a new question started bubbling up: who am I now?

In the beginning, everything revolved around not drinking. It was the mission, the anchor, the single goal that gave shape to my days. Don't drink. Avoid triggers. Stay connected. That focus got me through the hardest stretch. But somewhere into my second year, that clarity started to fade. The danger wasn't relapse. It was a kind of emotional drifting. If I wasn't just the guy trying to stay sober anymore, then who exactly was I?

I brought this up to Dr. Russell during a session around the fourteen-month mark. "I feel like I'm stuck in a weird in-between," I said. "The crisis is over, but now I'm not sure what comes next. And honestly, I feel like sobriety has become too much of my identity. It's all I talk about."

He didn't seem surprised. "Totally normal at this point," he said. "In early recovery, it's natural for sobriety to be front and center. But long-term recovery has to grow into something bigger. That's where the idea of 'recovery capital' comes in, building a life with meaning, purpose, and connection. Something to grow into, not just something to avoid."

The phrase stuck with me: recovery capital. I liked that it sounded solid, like something you could build brick by brick.

"But what does that even look like?" I asked. "What am I supposed to be building?"

Dr. Russell smiled and asked, "If you met someone new, how many sentences would it take before you mentioned that you're sober? And what would you say about yourself before that?"

That question hit harder than I expected. Over the last year, I had talked so much about quitting drinking, about the recovery process, about all the work it took to get here. I realized I wasn't totally sure how to talk about myself without starting there.

Yes, I was still a husband, a father, a data scientist. But those were roles I'd held before. Who was I now that sobriety wasn't consuming all my focus? What mattered to me beyond staying sober?

Dr. Russell put it this way: "You're not just rebuilding your relationship with alcohol. You're rebuilding your relationship with yourself."

That line stayed with me.

It's easy to skip these kinds of questions when alcohol is still in the picture. Drinking has a way of smoothing over the hard edges, blurring the uncomfortable stuff. Without it, those deeper, more human questions rise to the surface. What do I care about? What kind of man do I want to be? What kind of life do I want to live?

Sobriety didn't just remove a substance. It stripped away the fog that let me ignore those questions for years. And now, in the clarity, I was left to answer them for real.

As I moved deeper into my second year of sobriety, a new question took center stage. If I wasn't drinking, and I wasn't focused on not drinking every day, then who exactly was I now? What filled the space that alcohol used to occupy?

That search led me back to something I hadn't touched in decades: photography.

In high school and college, I'd been one of those guys who always had a camera slung over his shoulder. I wasn't amazing, but I loved it. I loved the quiet focus it required, the way it pulled me into the moment. But like a lot of things, it faded over time. Slowly, subtly, my free time and creative energy were swallowed by drinking. Before I even realized it, the camera was gathering dust.

Sixteen months into sobriety, on a random Thursday, I bought a new digital camera. Nothing flashy, just something solid enough to do the job. The next morning, I headed out early, before the city had really woken up, and started walking.

Those early-morning photo walks quickly became a ritual. They weren't about making art or building a portfolio. They were about seeing. About noticing the light hitting a fire escape just right or the symmetry in a row of empty cafe chairs. It became a kind of moving meditation, a way to shift my focus from the endless loop in my head to the world outside it.

When I got home, Sarah noticed the shift. "You always seem calmer after your photo mornings," she said one Sunday as I flipped through images on my laptop.

"It gets me out of my head," I told her. "I spend all day at work dissecting data. And since I got sober, I've spent so much time dissecting myself. Photography is the opposite. It's about just looking. Just seeing."

What surprised me most was how it connected me with Alex.

He was nine now, right in that middle space where he still wanted time with his parents, but was also discovering his own interests. One weekend in Central Park, I handed him the camera and showed him the basics: focus, shutter, and light.

When we got home and went through the photos, I was genuinely impressed. He had an instinct for it. He captured moments I hadn't even noticed.

"You've got a good eye," I told him.

"What does that mean?" he asked, scrunching his face in that way he does when he's trying to puzzle something out.

"It means you see things other people might miss. Patterns, little details."

He thought about that for a second. "Like you do with numbers?"

"Exactly," I said, smiling. "Just with pictures instead of data."

That became our thing. Nothing elaborate, just walks, a camera, and the simple act of paying attention. We didn't need a big plan or an event. We just needed to go out and look.

In a way, photography gave me back something I hadn't even realized I'd lost. Not just a creative outlet, but a way to be present. And in sharing it with Alex, I wasn't just rebuilding myself. I was building something new between us. Something rooted in curiosity, attention, and time. Things alcohol had long kept me from offering fully.

One of the biggest shifts in my second year of sobriety had nothing to do with alcohol. It had to do with what I used to think of as "normal."

For years, I had convinced myself that my drinking was perfectly reasonable. Normal, even. Just part of the routine for people in high-stress careers. Something you did to take the edge off or celebrate a win. Everyone I knew drank. It was part of the culture. I never stopped to question whether that "normal" was actually doing me any favors.

Quitting drinking forced me to look at that more honestly. Once I started pulling on that thread, the whole sweater of so-called normalcy started to unravel.

Was it actually normal to check email at midnight, every night? Was it normal to measure my self-worth by title and salary? Was it normal to go weeks without a real conversation that went beyond project updates or weekend plans? Was it normal to always feel like I was falling behind, even when I was technically succeeding?

One evening, maybe eighteen months into sobriety, I looked at Sarah over dinner and said, "I think I'm having a really late quarter-life crisis."

She raised an eyebrow. "You're forty six."

"Exactly," I said. "I'm finally questioning everything I used to just accept."

She didn't laugh. She just nodded and said, "That doesn't sound like a crisis. That sounds like clarity."

That word, clarity, stuck with me.

Sobriety hadn't just removed alcohol. It had removed the filter I had been living through. I was seeing things more clearly now, which was great, but also uncomfortable. It forced me to face some truths I had been sidestepping for a long time about work, ambition, and priorities.

Then came the promotion offer. Vice President. Big title, big team, big paycheck, and big expectations. More travel. Longer hours. Less margin for anything that didn't show up on a quarterly report.

Old me would have said yes before the offer even finished leaving the recruiter's mouth. I would have toasted it with scotch and booked a celebratory dinner. But now, I hesitated.

I talked it over with Sarah. I told her the details, the numbers, the scope of the new role. Then I admitted, "I know I should be thrilled. But mostly, I feel anxious. I keep thinking about what this would cost: time, energy, presence."

She didn't tell me what to do. Instead, she asked, "What does your gut say?"

I paused. "It says I want the growth, but not at the price of everything else."

Then she said something that, to this day, might be the most freeing thing I've heard in recovery. "You're allowed to have different priorities now. You're not the same person you were when you were drinking."

It hit me. Hard. I had spent a year and a half changing how I lived, but I hadn't fully updated how I defined success. I was still operating under the same set of expectations, just doing it sober. Maybe that wasn't enough.

So I didn't walk away from the role. But I didn't accept it as-is either. I negotiated a different version: less travel, tighter boundaries around nights and weekends, and yes, slightly less money. It wasn't easy to explain to colleagues, some of whom clearly thought I was playing small or being overly cautious.

But for me, it wasn't about playing small. It was about playing smart. It was about playing true. It was about building a life that could actually support the version of me I was trying to grow into, not the one I had been trying to drink away.

That was the real lesson of year two. Sobriety isn't just about quitting something. It's about building something better. It's about making deliberate choices, even when they don't look impressive on a resume. It's about saying, "That might be normal, but it's not for me anymore."

It's about finally getting clear, and then having the courage to live by what you see.

As I got closer to the two-year mark, I noticed something had shifted. It didn't happen in a sudden, dramatic way, but more like the way a season changes. Quietly, gradually, almost without notice, until one day you step outside and realize the air smells different.

Early sobriety felt like living inside a fire drill. Alarms blared, rules were everywhere, everything felt urgent and binary. No gray areas. No flexibility. That rigidity was necessary at the time. It kept me safe while I was rebuilt. By the second year, that black-and-white thinking started to soften. My commitment to staying sober remained solid, but the way sobriety fit into my life had changed. It didn't have to be the headline anymore.

I could be both a person in recovery and someone who enjoyed his work. I could carry the memory of addiction and also carry insight and value from what I had learned. Sobriety was still central, but it wasn't my whole identity. It was part of the foundation I was building everything else on.

That shift showed up in small moments. Like when a new client invited me for drinks after a meeting and I simply said, "I don't drink, but I'd be up for coffee or lunch." No long explanation. No awkwardness. Just a boundary, stated plainly.

Or when I showed up to a team happy hour. I didn't go to prove a point. I went because I felt like being there. I sipped sparkling water, talked shop, and left when I was ready. Other times, I didn't go at all. It wasn't because I was avoiding temptation, but because I was tired or wanted to be home with Sarah and Alex. The decision wasn't loaded anymore.

Even old friends, the ones who knew me during my heaviest drinking years, would ask, "Wait, you're still not drinking? I thought that was just a reset."

I would smile and say, "Yeah. It's working for me. I feel better than I have in years." That was enough.

Sobriety had become something I carried lightly. Not casually, but without the weight of constant explanation or defense. It was no longer this huge, looming story I told about myself. It was just part of who I was, like being a morning person or having bad knees. Something I considered when making decisions, but not something that needed to dominate every conversation or dictate every interaction.

Dr. Russell once described this phase as the shift from "emergency recovery" to "life practice." I loved that framing. The fire was out. The panic had subsided. The work continued, but it was quieter now and more sustainable. It wasn't about staying on high alert. It was about showing up every day with honesty and intention. It was about living in a way that didn't require escaping from myself.

That, I realized, was what made this part of the journey so rich. It wasn't flashy or dramatic. It was just steady. Grounded. Real.

Just as I had settled into a quieter, steadier rhythm with sobriety, life threw me one of those moments that splits time in two: before and after.

My dad died suddenly of a heart attack.

The call came on an ordinary Thursday afternoon. I stepped out of a meeting to answer the phone and heard my mother's trembling voice telling me he was gone. My knees buckled. I slid to the hallway floor, trying to process something my brain refused to understand. My father, strong and sharp, the guy who fixed everything, was just gone.

What followed was a blur: flying to Chicago, making funeral arrangements, seeing old faces, delivering a eulogy. Sarah and Alex arrived the next day and helped me hold it together. Through it all, I moved like someone operating underwater, present but muffled, just going through the motions.

It wasn't until the night after the funeral, sitting alone in the guest room, that the full weight of it landed. And with it came a craving I hadn't felt in over two years. It was not just a passing urge. This one hit like a freight train. It was visceral, almost physical. The thought came quickly and clearly: just one drink. No one would blame you. Not for this.

I sat there, trembling, staring at the ceiling, and texted Michael, my recovery buddy. I told him what had happened. I told him I wanted to drink. I told him I didn't think the tools I had were strong enough for this.

He called immediately. He didn't try to fix it. He just listened. When he finally spoke, it wasn't a lecture. It was simple. "This is what grief feels like without a buffer. It's supposed to hurt."

"But how do I get through it?" I asked. I felt like a beginner all over again.

"The same way you've gotten through everything else. One moment at a time," he said. Then he added something that stayed with me: "Maybe staying sober through this is a way of honoring your dad."

That changed something in me. My dad was a man who showed up for everything. He did not run from hard stuff. Maybe the best way I could honor him was by doing the same.

That night I didn't drink. I sat with the grief and let it tear through me. Somehow, I woke up the next day still sober.

The months that followed were not easier. Grief came in waves. Sometimes it was sadness, sometimes it was anger, sometimes it was just numbness. Still, I didn't drink. Not because I had all the answers. Not because I felt strong. But because I had made a decision to feel everything life gave me, even when it hurt.

Sobriety didn't protect me from the pain. But it let me be present. For my mom. For Sarah and Alex. For myself. I remembered my dad with clarity. I helped pack up his things. I laughed at old stories and cried at unexpected songs. I did all of it clear-headed.

When my third sobriety anniversary came, eight months after he died, I didn't feel triumphant. I felt grateful. Grateful for the presence, for the resilience, and for the chance to live life as it comes: unfiltered, unedited, and real.

Sobriety, it turned out, was not just about avoiding alcohol. It was about choosing to show up. Even when it hurts. Especially when it hurts. That, more than anything, felt like the kind of life my dad would have been proud of.

Exactly three years after my last drink, I found myself sitting alone on a bench in Prospect Park. Morning light filtered softly through the spring leaves. I hadn't come for a celebration or to check a box. I came to think, to breathe, and to take in the view of the park. More than that, I wanted to look back over the past twenty-four months.

The man who sat trembling on the bathroom floor two years earlier, convinced he was dying, body unraveling, mind in panic, felt like a ghost I barely recognized. It was not because some miracle had turned me into someone new overnight. It happened because so many quiet changes added up to something solid and real.

The physical stuff was easy to spot. I was down twenty pounds. My face looked sharper. The puffiness around my eyes was long gone. My resting heart rate had dropped by twenty beats. The morning tremor I used to chalk up to stress had disappeared without fanfare. But the deeper changes, the ones that actually mattered, could not be seen in the mirror.

The constant anxiety of my drinking years, the pressure to perform, the mental fog, the fear I'd said something I couldn't remember, and the gnawing worry about my health had faded. Not all at once, but slowly, like fog lifting from a windshield. And emotionally, I did not live on the same edge anymore. I could feel things, whether grief, frustration, or joy, without tipping into chaos.

My marriage had changed too. Sarah stuck with me through the worst of it. She did not do it with blind loyalty, but with clear-eyed love. She hadn't coddled me, but she hadn't abandoned me either. Sobriety demanded honesty, and that honesty deepened our trust in ways nothing else could have.

Then there was Alex. Nearly eleven now. He would never know the version of me who missed bedtime stories because he had passed out on the couch. He would not remember the dad who made promises he couldn't keep because of what he drank the night before. What he would know instead was a dad who showed up, who listened, who followed through. That alone felt like reason enough to stay sober for the rest of my life.

Work looked different, too. I was no longer charging through projects on a mix of adrenaline and self-doubt. I was not covering up the night before with extra emails and energy drinks. I led more calmly now, more clearly. And my team noticed. Not because I pushed harder, but because I was steadier. Present. Human.

None of these changes came from some dramatic turning point. They were the result of a thousand little decisions. Every day, every hour, I chose to stay on course. It was not just about avoiding drinking, but about living in a way that no longer needed it.

Sitting on that bench, watching the sunlight dance through the trees, I didn't feel triumphant. I felt grateful. Not just for what was gone—hangovers, shame, the never-ending mind games—but for what had taken its place. I was grateful for the chance to be awake for my own life, to be present, for Sarah, for Alex, and for myself.

Three years sober did not feel like a finish line. It did not even feel like a destination. It was a moment to pause and recognize the ground I had covered. It was a time to remember that the road ahead was not about staying the same, but continuing to grow.

I stood up and started walking home. Sarah and Alex would be waking soon. There would be coffee and some small conversation about school lunches or meetings or weekend plans. Nothing big. Just another Tuesday. And that was the real gift. Another clear-eyed, ordinary day. Another chance to live this one well.

Three years in, the journey had not ended. It had just begun.

Chapter Eleven

When Everything Goes Wrong

S OME YEARS HAVE PASSED. Now I do not even keep track of how many days, months, or years I have been sober. Life simply moves forward. Somewhere along the way, counting felt less important than living.

By my seventh year of sobriety, I found myself believing I had finally built a foundation that could not be shaken. I'd survived the storms that used to sink me: grief, work stress, and family arguments. After all of that, drinking never even crossed my mind as a solution. My confidence grew slowly. Maybe I was even a bit smug about it, telling myself I'd finally figured life out.

That feeling lasted right up until a Monday morning in March, when the ground dropped out from under me.

It started with my usual routine. I was in my office, knee-deep in quarterly reports, when my assistant came to the door, looking rattled. "Dave, there are two FBI agents here. They want to talk to you." It landed like a punch. The FBI. In my building. I could see other employees sneaking looks, pretending to work while two men in suits stood at reception.

I managed to keep my voice steady. "Okay. Send them to conference room B."

The next three hours were a blur. Easily the longest and hardest of my career. They told me our company had been hacked. Not just any breach, but a devastating one. Client lists, financials, proprietary code, all gone. Stolen by someone who clearly knew their way around the system. An inside job, most likely.

"Mr. Halston," said Agent Martinez, sliding a file toward me, "you had access to everything that was compromised. Can you account for your logins in the last six months?"

I answered as best I could, but every question made me feel smaller. They'd traced some suspicious logins to my credentials. My own laptop showed strange network activity. And then came the cherry on top: a few old coworkers had raised concerns about my "instability" during my drinking days.

"We're not charging you," Agent Chen said, "but you need to understand. This is serious. Corporate espionage can mean real prison time."

Prison. The word echoed as I left the room. By lunch, everyone at the company knew something was wrong. Folks who used to chat with me at the coffee machine suddenly found other things to do. My access was suspended "pending the investigation." Technically, I still had a job, but I was basically in limbo.

Driving home, my mind kept running in circles. How was I supposed to explain all this to Sarah? I rehearsed a dozen versions of the conversation, none of them good. But when I opened the door, she was already on the phone, her voice tense, almost frantic.

"Yes, I understand," she was saying, "but we can't do anything until we confirm what's making them sick."

She hung up and sank into a chair. Before I could get a word out, she told me what was happening: a possible outbreak at the hospital. Three kids, all with the same strange neurological symptoms, maybe some kind of poisoning. She'd be pulling eighteen-hour shifts until they figured it out.

I hesitated, not sure whether to pile on. But the news was too big to hold. "Sarah, I need to tell you something. The FBI came to my office."

She looked up, exhausted. "What?"

So I told her the whole story: the hack, the investigation, the fact that, for now, I was the prime suspect. I watched the disbelief on her face give way to a kind of numb worry.

"I want to be there for you," she said, "but I can't walk away from the hospital. These kids." She didn't finish the sentence, but I got it. She was torn in two. "You've handled big stuff before, Dave. Seven years of tools, right?"

Seven years of tools. That line echoed in my mind as I tried to sleep that night. I'd built a toolkit for cravings, stress, loss, but nothing for this.

The next morning, it somehow got worse. I woke up to three urgent emails. Three of our biggest clients had cut ties overnight. Word was out: there was a federal investigation, and my name was floating around in the rumors. By noon, my phone wouldn't stop. Reporters wanted statements about an alleged insider trading ring, which was news to me. It all felt surreal, like I was watching my life slide off a cliff in slow motion.

Then, as I was doom-scrolling the latest headlines, my phone rang. School number. Never a good sign.

"Mr. Halston, this is Principal Rodriguez. We need you to come in right away. Alex has been caught with a vaping device, and he wasn't truthful about how he got it."

I sat in my car outside the school for a long minute, forehead on the steering wheel. My thirteen-year-old, messing around with substances, while I was being threatened with prison. You really can't make this stuff up.

Inside, Principal Rodriguez explained the story. Alex had denied it, then said a friend gave it to him, then finally admitted he bought it from another kid. The dishonesty, the principal said, was as serious as the vaping itself. I glanced over at Alex, arms crossed, eyes on the floor, silent and defiant. It was like looking in a time machine at myself, the first time I got caught sneaking a beer as a teenager.

On the drive home, we didn't say a word. I just kept thinking, How do I even start to parent through this? How do you talk about honesty and substance use when your own life is splashed all over the news, and your past isn't exactly a clean slate?

Back at the house, I tried to sit him down.

"Alex, we need to talk about what happened," I said.

He barely looked up. "I know. Vaping is bad. Lying is bad. Can I go now?"

"No," I said, keeping my voice calm. "This isn't just about the rules. You need to know something real about our family."

For the first time, I told him more of the truth. Addiction ran in our blood. I'd struggled with it. It's not something we can ignore. He listened, but I could see the skepticism in his eyes.

"So because you had a drinking problem, I can't try anything?" he shot back.

"That's not it. I'm saying you have to be careful. You need to be honest about it, too."

He didn't miss a beat. "You lied about your drinking. Mom told me."

That landed hard. He was right. I'd spent years covering things up, spinning stories, pretending. Who was I to act holier-than-thou now?

I was still searching for words when my phone rang again. My mother's number.

"David, honey, I didn't want to worry you, but I'm at the hospital. I fell and broke my hip. They want to do surgery."

She tried to sound tough, but I could hear the fear in her voice. Since my dad died, she'd worked so hard not to be a burden. But now she was alone in Chicago, scared, and pretending she'd be fine.

I promised I'd come, even though I didn't know how I'd manage it, with the investigation, with Sarah pulled into a hospital crisis, and Alex acting out.

That night, Sarah finally came home close to midnight, scrubs still on, hair a mess. She sank into the couch, and I filled her in on everything: Alex and the vaping, my mom's surgery, the investigation swallowing up my career. I heard myself rattling off the list, spiraling, every problem stacked on the last.

She cut me off. "Dave, stop. This is more than anyone should have to juggle. We need to pick what matters most right now."

She was right. But it all felt connected—the job, the money, my mom's medical bills, Alex's behavior, the pressure on our family. Every crisis seemed to feed the next.

"I can't leave the hospital," she said, "but you should go to your mom. Alex can come with me after school for a few days. Maybe seeing the real stuff at the hospital will snap him out of it."

At least it was a plan. But as I lay in bed, staring at the ceiling, I felt a wave I hadn't felt in years: a craving so strong it made perfect sense. My brain served up the old answer. Just one drink. One to take the edge off, a few to finally let me sleep, half a bottle to numb the panic for one night.

And for the first time since I got sober, the thought didn't scare me. It felt almost reasonable. Like this was the one situation my sobriety toolkit hadn't prepared me for.

The next morning, I called my lawyer, the same one who had handled my father's estate, and told him what was happening. He didn't hesitate. He put me in touch with a criminal defense attorney who knew his way around white-collar cases.

"Do not talk to the FBI without someone in the room," he said. "And do not discuss the case with anyone, not even your family. Anything you say could be dragged into this later."

So there I was, carrying this huge secret. I couldn't even process it with Sarah because, if things went sideways, she might get pulled in as a witness.

Traveling to Chicago felt as bumpy as my life at that point. The flight was rough. I sat in 14B, gripping the armrests, stomach in knots, and fighting the urge to flag down the flight attendant for a whiskey. Just one small bottle to take the edge off. That was all I wanted before I had to walk into my mom's hospital room and figure out everything from her surgery to how she'd get groceries over the next month.

Instead, I ordered a ginger ale and tried to remember my therapist's breathing exercises. It felt useless, like using a paper towel to mop up a flood.

Seeing my mom in that hospital bed knocked the air out of me. She looked older than the last time I'd seen her, smaller, her gray hair fanned out across the pillow. But her mind was as sharp as ever. She took one look at me and saw through everything.

"You look terrible, David. What's really going on?"

I gave her a version that left out all the worst parts. I told her work was rough and there were some legal headaches, but that things would sort themselves out. I couldn't drop my entire burden on her, not with her facing surgery.

The operation itself went as planned, but recovery would be a long haul. She needed help with just about everything: physical therapy, daily chores, rides to appointments. I spent three days juggling her care, lining up home health aides, making charts for her medications, getting her set up for grocery delivery.

All the while, my phone buzzed nonstop. Back in New York, more clients were jumping ship. Another news story popped up, speculating about my supposed role in the investigation. A few old work friends sent awkward messages, and a few more just vanished. The world I'd built seemed to be falling apart in real time.

On top of that, there was Alex. Every update from Sarah made my stomach twist. "Caught him lying about where he was after school." "He's hanging out with older kids." "His attitude is getting worse." Each message was like watching a car crash. You can't stop knowing your kid is drifting into the same trouble you once did, and you're too far away to help.

The breaking point came late Thursday night. I was in my mother's living room, surrounded by a mess of medical bills and insurance papers, when Sarah called.

"Dave, I need you to come home. Now."

I sat up straight. "What happened?"

Her voice was tight. "Alex didn't come home from school. When I finally found him, he'd been drinking with high school kids in the park. He's not drunk, but he has definitely been drinking. And when I asked him why, he said..." She stopped, then her voice broke. "He said maybe he should just follow in your footsteps."

Those words landed like a punch to the gut. My thirteen-year-old, drinking in a park, using my own story as his excuse.

"I'll catch the first flight out," I said.

"Your mom..." she started.

"She has health aides and neighbors. Alex is my priority," I said, already opening my laptop to find a ticket home.

As I sat there, trying to book a red-eye back to New York, it all came crashing down. The criminal investigation hanging over my head. My career, probably gone for good. My mother, hurt and alone in a hospital bed. My son, starting down the same path I once walked. Sarah, pulled in every direction, left to hold everything together.

Seven years of sobriety, seven years of building tools and learning new ways to cope, and none of it seemed to matter now.

I left the house and walked to the corner liquor store three blocks away. The neon sign in the window buzzed in the darkness: "Beer Wine Spirits." Inside, I went straight to the whiskey, grabbed a bottle of Jameson, and felt the weight of it in my hand. It was almost a comfort, as familiar as an old friend.

The clerk rang me up without even looking at me. Just another customer buying a bottle late at night.

Back at my mother's kitchen table, I set the bottle down and stared at it. Unopened, but full of possibility. I could have a drink. Maybe two. Just enough to steady myself so I could think straight and get through the next few days. I told myself that seven years sober should have taught me something about moderation.

I twisted off the cap. The smell was as familiar as ever: oak, honey, sharp and biting. My body remembered it, and for the first time in days, my hands stopped shaking.

For an hour I sat there, sometimes lifting the bottle to my lips, sometimes putting it down. The urge was more than just mental. It was like gravity, pulling me closer.

But each time I almost drank, I thought of Alex. I thought of the phone call I'd have to make to Sarah if I caved. I thought of facing the FBI, and the shame of admitting I'd thrown away my sobriety when everything else was falling apart. Most of all, I thought about the person I'd become since that first day on the bathroom floor seven years ago. I wasn't perfect, but I'd become someone who didn't run. Someone who faced what was in front of him.

If I drank now, I'd show my son that the way to survive pain is to escape. I'd be teaching him to run when things get hard. But if I stayed sober, I might show him something different: that you can live through the hardest days without numbing out, that you can be scared and still stand your ground.

So I picked up the bottle, carried it to the sink, and poured every drop down the drain. Watching it swirl away, I felt both weak and strong at the same time.

Then I picked up the phone and called my sponsor, Michael. I hadn't talked to him in months.

"I almost drank tonight," I said. "For the first time in seven years, I really wanted to."

"But you didn't," he replied. "That's what counts. What kept you from it?"

I paused for a moment. "My son. And not wanting to lose who I've become."

He was quiet for a second, then said, "You lost nothing tonight. You decided who you want to be in a crisis. That's what really matters."

I flew back to New York the next morning with a clear head and a plan. Not a plan to solve everything. There was no way to do that, but at least a plan to face each mess one step at a time, staying present through all of it.

Talking to Alex was the hardest conversation I'd ever had with him. He was upset and prickly, defensive about being caught drinking and more embarrassed than he'd ever admit.

"You're such a hypocrite," he said. "You drank for like twenty years, and now you're mad at me for trying it once?"

"I'm not angry that you tried it," I told him. "I'm worried about the lying. I'm worried about why you tried it. Were you trying to deal with stress? Trying to feel older? Did you just want to fit in with those kids?"

He wouldn't meet my eyes. Just shrugged.

"That was exactly why I started drinking in high school. I wanted to fit in. And what started there almost ruined my life."

"Maybe I'm not like you," he shot back, still trying to put up a wall.

"Maybe you're not," I said. "But maybe you are. Either way, you deserve better than finding out the hard way."

Over the next few days, we had more honest conversations than we'd ever managed before. We talked about addiction, about our family history, about the pressure he was under at school. I didn't

THE DOUBLE LIFE OF A HIGH-FUNCTIONING ALCOHOLIC

hide the investigation or what it could mean for us as a family. I told him the truth: sometimes life throws more at you than feels fair, and you have to choose how you're going to respond.

The real turning point came when he finally asked me, "Were you scared when you quit drinking?"

"I was terrified," I told him. "Every day for months. I didn't know who I'd be without it."

"Are you scared now? About the FBI and everything?"

"Yes," I said. "But I'm still handling it. That's what adults do."

He nodded. I saw something in him shift. "Drinking wasn't fun, anyway. It just made me feel sick and stupid."

"Good," I said. "It should feel that way at thirteen. If it felt good, I'd be even more worried."

With Sarah tied up at the hospital, most of the discipline fell to me. Grounding Alex felt small compared to the risk he'd taken. So we made a plan together. He would go to a few AA meetings with me. He'd see a counselor who specialized in teens. After school, he'd spend his afternoons at the library, where I could pick him up on my way home. No more unsupervised time with the wrong crowd.

"This is a lot," he complained.

"It is a lot," I said. "Trying alcohol at thirteen is a big deal in our family. If you want adult choices, you get adult consequences."

Meanwhile, the FBI investigation kept rolling. My lawyer coached me through every interview, reminding me to keep my answers simple and clear. It was exhausting, but staying sober turned out to be crucial. My mind stayed sharp. I remembered details that might have been lost otherwise. I could handle the stress without the paranoia or confusion that comes with drinking.

Three weeks into the chaos, something unexpected happened. I was reviewing server logs late at night, hoping for anything that could help my case, when I spotted something odd. The login times did not match up with my calendar. There were access attempts when I was at company events, proven by sign-in sheets and photos. There were also strange patterns in where the logins seemed to come from. They made little sense if I was the one logging in.

I called my lawyer right away and stayed up all night documenting every inconsistency. By sunrise, I had enough proof to suggest someone had been using my credentials, picking times when I was clearly somewhere else to cover their tracks.

The FBI's tech team confirmed it fast. Within two days, they had their real suspect, a contractor who had been quietly stealing client data and selling it to competitors.

Agent Martinez called me with the update. "You are no longer a person of interest in this investigation. Your analysis helped us catch the real culprit. Thank you for your cooperation."

The relief was real, but it was mixed with something heavier. I kept thinking back to that bottle of Jameson in my mother's kitchen. If I had drunk again, would I have noticed the little details in those logs? Would I have thought as clearly or acted as quickly? I could not shake the thought that sobriety had saved more than my health this time.

Life did not magically return to normal. My reputation still needed time to recover. Some clients were still spooked by the investigation. My mother needed ongoing care, and Alex was still working through his own challenges with the help of a counselor.

But something inside me had changed. I had survived the worst storm of my adult life. I had stayed sober, not because it was easy, but because I chose to be present, even when escape seemed like the smartest option.

When the hospital finally got its outbreak under control, Sarah could pay attention to home again. One evening, after dinner, she sat across from me while Alex did his homework at the kitchen table.

"You handled all this so differently than before," she said. "You did not run from the problem. You stuck with it, even when it was at its hardest."

She was right. The old me would have tried to numb out. This time, I stayed awake through every moment, felt every feeling, and kept showing up for the people who needed me.

I called out to Alex. "What did you think of how Dad handled everything?"

He looked up from his math worksheet and thought for a second. "You didn't fall apart," he said. "Even when I thought you might. You just dealt with it."

That was the best compliment sobriety ever gave me. Not that I avoided alcohol, but that I stayed present when it mattered most.

Seven years sober, I faced the ultimate test. Everything that could go wrong did go wrong, but I learned something I never knew about myself. I was strong enough to make it through. Not because I was perfect, but because I learned to stay present, even in the middle of the storm.

The crisis eventually passed, as they always do. The confidence I gained by staying sober through it all? That was mine to keep.

Six months later, life had settled into a new kind of normal. My reputation bounced back, thanks in part to the fact that my detective work helped solve the real crime. Alex was making progress in counseling, and there had been no more run-ins with alcohol or anything else. My mom was back on her feet and living on her own again, with a little help from support services.

The biggest shift, though, was inside me. I no longer saw sobriety as something that might fail me when life got rough. I had learned it was exactly what I needed when everything went sideways. Sobriety was not some shield that kept trouble away. It was the ground I stood on to deal with it.

When people asked how I stayed sober through that storm, I always told them the truth. It was difficult. There was a moment when I came close to slipping. But I realized that drinking would not solve a single problem. It would just mean having to face those problems while drunk.

And I knew Alex was paying attention. He was watching how I handled a crisis. He was seeing what real strength looks like.

That meant more than any short-term relief a drink could have given me.

Seven years sober, I thought I had recovery all figured out. I see now. That was just the beginning.

Chapter Twelve

The Quiet Revolution

E IGHT YEARS INTO SOBRIETY, I unexpectedly found myself restless, even though I had everything I thought I wanted.

On paper, my life looked better than ever. My career not only recovered from the FBI ordeal, it actually got a boost. People respected me for staying calm and clear-headed under pressure, and new opportunities kept coming. My marriage was strong in a way that just was not possible during my drinking years. Alex was fifteen, doing well in school, playing varsity soccer, and there were no more substance scares. We had faced every storm life sent our way, and I stayed sober through it all.

But on a quiet Wednesday afternoon, sitting in my office, I realized I felt empty in a way I had not in years. It was not the old darkness from when I drank. This was something quieter. A sense that I was missing something important.

I had already proved I could stay sober. I had shown I could handle tough times and rebuild trust. I had put my family back together and earned my place at work. So why did it feel like I was still waiting for something to start?

That question followed me home. At dinner, Sarah picked up on my mood.

"You've seemed distant lately," she said after Alex went upstairs to do homework. "Are you alright?"

I tried to put words to it, but it sounded messy. "I am grateful for where we are. Really. But I keep wondering if there is more to this than just not drinking. What is the point of recovery if it is just about keeping things going the way they are?"

Sarah stirred her tea, thinking it over. "Maybe it is not about what you get from being sober anymore. Maybe it is about what you can give because you are sober."

Her words echoed in my mind as I did the dishes. What can I give because I am sober? I had spent years using recovery to fix my own life, to be a better husband, a better dad, to do my job well. But maybe there was something more. Maybe these eight years had prepared me for something I had never thought about.

The answer came sooner than I expected, and from a direction I never saw coming.

"Can I ask you something personal?"

The question came from Jamie, one of our newer data scientists. He had joined the team about six months back. We were getting coffee after a stressful client meeting, and I could hear something serious in his voice.

"Of course," I said, settling into a worn leather chair at the cafe.

Jamie fiddled with his cup for a bit, searching for the right words. "I've noticed you never drink at work events. And you always seem so steady. Like nothing shakes you up the way it does the rest of us."

I waited, giving him space. He was building up to something.

He finally spoke again, quieter this time. "The thing is, I think I might have a problem with alcohol. And I honestly don't know what to do."

His words hung there. For a moment, I saw my younger self across the table. Successful on the outside, but lost and scared underneath. Trying to hold it all together and ashamed to admit it was slipping away.

"What makes you think you have a problem?" I asked.

He started talking, and the details were all too familiar. Drinking to manage nerves at work events. Needing alcohol to unwind after tough days. Promises to cut back, broken almost right away. Blackouts, missed deadlines, the uneasy realization that drinking was no longer fun. It was starting to feel like a requirement.

"Everyone here drinks," he said, finally. "It's just part of the culture. If I admit I can't handle it, I feel like I'm admitting I can't handle the job."

I understood. I used to feel the same way. In this industry, admitting you struggle with alcohol feels like confessing a professional weakness, maybe even career suicide.

"Let me tell you something," I said. "I've been sober for eight years."

Jamie's eyes got big. "Really? But you seem so normal."

I laughed. "That was my biggest fear about quitting. I thought I'd lose my place, lose my ability to blend in. Turns out, I'm a lot more normal now than I ever was when I was drinking."

We sat together for another hour. I shared some of my story, careful not to lecture. I gave him the number for the treatment center where I used to go to meetings. I told him he was not alone, and that realizing you can't handle alcohol is not a weakness. It's actually a sign you are paying attention.

Three weeks later, he sent me a text. "Day ten. Thanks for showing me it was possible."

That message lit something up inside me. It brought back a sense of purpose I had not felt since those early days of sobriety, when every day felt like a victory. But this was different. It was not about my survival anymore. It was about helping someone else find their own way out.

I started to look around differently at work. I noticed who was always holding a drink at events, who came in looking rough on Monday mornings, who kept missing early meetings after company parties. I was not judging them. I just saw them—because I had been in their shoes.

When it felt right, I would share a bit of my own experience. Never in a dramatic way, just enough so they knew they were not alone. Just making myself quietly available, the way I once wished someone had done for me.

The invitation to volunteer at the recovery center came from a contact in my old support group. They were looking for people with professional backgrounds to help newly sober folks handle challenges at work.

"You wouldn't be a counselor," Patricia, the program director, told me when we first spoke. "We already have licensed professionals for that. What we need is someone who has been through it. Someone who can help people believe it's possible to rebuild a career, manage work relationships, and handle stress. All without drinking."

The work humbled me. Sometimes it broke my heart. But it was also beautiful in ways I didn't expect. I met people from every walk of life, all with the same kinds of battles I had faced. There were construction workers worried about job sites where drinking was part of the culture. Teachers who admitted to hiding flasks in their desks. Executives who had built entire careers around wine tastings and bourbon clubs.

Most days, my main job was to listen. Sometimes I'd share a tip that had helped me, or offer my perspective if someone wanted it. But what really seemed to matter was just being proof that recovery is possible without giving up your ambition or your social life.

One night, after a tough group session, a woman named Maria pulled me aside.

"Eight years ago, I was making six figures as a pharmaceutical sales rep," she said. "Now I'm two months sober, working retail, because I lost everything. Sometimes I wonder if it's worth it."

I took a moment before answering. "I can't decide that for you. But I can tell you that the person I am now—at work, at home, everywhere—is someone I actually like. That was never true when I was drinking, no matter how good things looked from the outside."

She looked at me for a long time, then asked, "How long did it take before you actually believed that?"

"It took more than two months," I said. "But not eight years, either. Somewhere along the way, you stop pretending to be okay and actually start feeling okay."

Six months later, Maria sent me a message on LinkedIn. She had landed a job in pharmaceutical research, bought her own small apartment, and was celebrating eight months sober. She wrote, "Thank you for showing me what 'actually okay' can look like."

Those moments changed me. Each conversation, every small win, and every text from someone marking another milestone started to fill the restless feeling I'd carried. This was why sobriety mattered. Not just to keep myself stable, but to be useful to others still fighting to find their way out.

The changes at home were quieter, but just as meaningful. Alex was fifteen now, and he had started asking tougher questions, the ones I knew would come, but still felt a little unprepared for.

One night after soccer practice, as I was driving him home, he just came out with it. "Dad, am I going to be an alcoholic?"

His tone was so straightforward that I had to fight the urge to brush it off with some easy reassurance.

"I don't know," I told him. "You do have some risk factors, and you've seen how addiction can play out in our family. But that doesn't mean you're destined for it. There are people with a family history who never have any trouble, and there are people with no history who still end up with problems."

He looked out the window, thinking. After a minute he said, "Would you be disappointed if I never drank at all?"

That one surprised me. "Disappointed? Why would I be disappointed?"

He shrugged. "I don't know. You figured out how to drink normally now, right? Maybe you'd want me to learn that too."

I pulled into the driveway and left the engine running. I didn't want to rush this conversation.

"Alex, I never figured out how to drink normally. What I figured out was how to live normally without drinking. There's a big difference."

He was quiet, then asked, "But don't you miss it sometimes?"

I gave it some real thought. "There are things I miss. It made social stuff easier. It took the edge off sometimes. But I don't miss the person I was when I was drinking, and I don't miss the way it affected us as a family."

He nodded, slow and thoughtful. "The kids at school think it's weird not to drink."

"Some adults think it's weird, too. But here's something I've learned. The people who say sobriety is strange are usually the ones who should probably take a closer look at their own drinking."

He looked over at me. "Is that why you help other people quit?"

That caught me off guard. I'd tried to keep my volunteer work pretty low-key.

"How did you know about that?"

He smirked a little. "I hear you on the phone sometimes. And Mom told me you help people at work who are going through what you went through."

Sarah and I had promised to be honest with Alex about my recovery, but I hadn't realized he was paying such close attention.

"Yeah, I do what I can. Why?"

He shrugged again. "I think it's cool. You don't make it a big deal, but you help people. That's the kind of person I want to be."

That conversation stuck with me for days. My fifteen-year-old was watching. Not just the way I lived, but the way I showed up for others. The work I was doing for myself and for others was making an impact bigger than I'd ever planned.

The official opportunity arrived about six months later, right when I least expected it. Rebecca from HR called me into what I thought was a standard check-in. She sat down across from me and got right to the point.

"Dave, I want to run something by you," she said. "We're planning to expand our Employee Assistance Program, especially for mental health and substance use support. Your background has come up in our conversations."

Even with eight years of sobriety behind me, a wave of anxiety hit. I still worried sometimes about what being open about my addiction might mean for my career.

"In what way?" I asked, keeping my tone neutral.

"We're thinking about having you lead the new initiative. We need someone who understands both the clinical realities and the workplace culture. Someone who has navigated these issues personally and can talk about recovery in a real, honest way."

She slid a folder over to me. "It's a new role: Director of Workplace Wellness. Officially, it's a lateral move, same pay, similar level of responsibility, but the focus is totally different. You'd be building programs, training managers, creating resources, maybe even speaking at conferences."

I glanced at the job description inside the folder. It was all the work I'd been doing informally, but now with a real title and support behind it.

"There's one other thing," Rebecca said. "We'd want you to be open about your own recovery as part of the role. Not turning your story into a sales pitch, but sharing it when it makes sense. The credibility would mean a lot to the program."

That evening, I brought it up with Sarah over dinner. Alex was at the table, supposedly doing homework, but I knew he was listening in.

Sarah did not hesitate. "It sounds perfect for you. You're already doing this on the side. Now you'd have more resources and a bigger platform."

I hesitated. "It's a big shift. I'd be leaving the technical work I've done for fifteen years. And everyone would know about my history with addiction."

Alex piped up from the other side of the room. "Is that bad?"

We both looked at him.

He shrugged. "Being known for helping people sounds better than being known for data models."

It was a moment of clarity. Leave it to a teenager to see what really matters.

Sarah brought up another point. "Will this kind of work be too emotionally draining? Being around people who are struggling every day?"

I'd thought about that too, but my experience with volunteering had surprised me. Instead of feeling worn down by other people's stories, I felt more energized. Each time I helped someone, I was reminded of how far I'd come. It kept my own recovery strong.

"I actually think it would make me better at staying sober," I said. "Helping people who are fighting for their sobriety reminds me why mine is worth protecting."

Three weeks later, I found myself back in the bathroom of that same Manhattan hotel where I had once hidden my shaking hands. This time, I was there for a routine reason. A quick stop during a break at a wellness conference. I was there to learn more about best practices for the new workplace program.

But standing at the sink, washing my hands, I could not help but notice the symbolism. Eight years ago, I stood in this very spot, terrified my coworkers would notice I was in withdrawal, doing everything I could to hide the evidence of my drinking. I was sure my career would be over if anyone figured out the truth.

Now I was here as someone who helps others face the same struggles I once kept hidden. My recovery was not just something I kept quiet about. It was the reason I was qualified for this new role.

It felt surreal. Not only was I still sober, but the meaning of recovery in my life had completely changed. What used to be my secret shame had turned into my biggest source of purpose.

As I left the bathroom, my phone buzzed with a text from Jamie, the young data scientist I had helped months earlier. He wrote, "One year sober today. I'm starting to help a coworker who's where I was last year. Thanks for showing me how this works."

Reading that message, I felt something settle inside me. This was how recovery is supposed to work. Not as something you protect alone, but as something you pass on. Jamie was now helping someone else. That person would likely do the same for someone down the road. The healing kept moving outward, farther than I could ever reach on my own.

This was what the last eight years had been about. It was never just about my own sobriety. It was about being useful to others still looking for a way out of the darkness.

Six months after starting the new role, I was invited to speak at a national conference focused on workplace mental health. The audience included HR directors, EAP coordinators, and occupational health professionals. Many of them supported people dealing with addiction and mental health issues, but not all of them had lived through it themselves.

I had done presentations before, but this one felt different. It was more personal, more vulnerable, and more important than anything I had delivered in the past.

I opened with a story I had never shared publicly. I described the night I sat in my mother's kitchen with an open bottle of whiskey, right in the middle of the worst crisis of my sobriety, and how I decided to pour it down the drain instead of drinking it.

"I share this story," I told the three hundred professionals in the room, "not because I am proud that I almost relapsed, but because I want you to see something about the people your programs are meant to help. These are not weak people. They do not lack willpower. They are fighting a daily battle, and sometimes they just need help to remember why the fight matters."

I talked about why addiction needs to be treated as a health condition and not a character flaw. I spoke about building workplace cultures where people feel safe reaching out for help before things fall apart. I pointed out that companies benefit when they support employees in recovery, instead of waiting for problems to spiral.

But what I spoke about most was the quiet revolution that starts when people in recovery begin helping others. This shift can change not just individual lives, but entire communities.

During the Q&A, a woman in the front row raised her hand.

"This is a bit personal," she said, "but I have been concerned about my own drinking. Nothing dramatic, but there are patterns that worry me. What would you say to someone who is just beginning to wonder if she needs help?"

The room went silent. This was not a policy question or a clinical debate. This was someone reaching out for herself.

"I would tell you that just asking that question is important," I said. "Most people who do not have a problem never even wonder if they might. I would also say you do not have to figure it out alone. There are resources and help available, and asking for support is smart, not weak."

After my talk, she waited until the room was empty before coming up to thank me. I gave her some resources, including the name of a counselor who works with professionals starting recovery.

Three months later, she emailed me to say, "Ninety days sober. Your talk may have saved my life."

It is these moments. The quiet conversations, the personal follow-ups, and the knowledge that my story was giving others permission to change. Those moments have reshaped my sense of purpose. Recovery was never just about getting my own life back. It was about using my second chance to help others take theirs back, too.

On the eight-year anniversary of my sobriety, I did not throw a party or spend much time looking back. I spent the day the same way I spend most days now, by putting my energy toward something bigger than myself.

That morning, I sat across from a marketing executive who was three months sober and trying to figure out how to handle business trips without slipping up. In the afternoon, I went through applications for our company's new recovery support program. That evening, I joined a group at the volunteer center, helping other professionals who were early in their recovery journeys.

Each part of my day was a reminder of the distance I have traveled. It also reminded me that the work of recovery is never really finished. Recovery is not a finish line you cross and then rest. It is a path you walk, day by day. The real privilege now is that I get to walk it alongside others who are trying to find their way.

One evening, Alex, now fifteen and always thinking about big questions, asked me what mattered most from my eight years of sobriety.

I paused before answering. "I think the most important thing I have learned is that recovery is not really about me anymore. At the start, it had to be. I needed to get my feet under me first. But the real value is what sobriety allows me to give to other people. The purpose comes from being able to help someone else believe that change is possible."

He nodded and went back to his homework, but I kept thinking about his question as I got ready for bed.

Eight years ago, I was just trying to stay alive. I could not see past my own pain. I never guessed that my fight for sobriety would grow into something bigger—that I would end up helping others find their way out, too.

The quiet revolution of recovery does not make headlines. It does not happen through grand gestures or dramatic stories. It happens in honest conversations over coffee, in simple acts of service, and in showing up for others, over and over again. This is how you show people, and yourself, that hope is possible and that survival is not the end of the story.

After eight years, I finally understood what all of this was for. Recovery is not just about reclaiming your own life. It is about taking the hardest parts of your past and using them to light the path for someone else who still feels lost.

That is the gift of sobriety: being able to turn your biggest struggle into real purpose. Being able to help rebuild lives, starting with your own, then reaching out to others.

The quiet revolution goes on, one conversation at a time, one act of kindness at a time, one life at a time.

This is the life I never expected to have. I built it on the foundation of the life I almost lost. And now I see. It is exactly the life I needed all along.

Chapter Thirteen

Letter to My Drinking Self

H EY DAVE,
      You don't know me yet, but I know you. I know
where you are right now. You are sitting on that cold bathroom
floor at 2:37 AM, heart pounding like it's trying to break free,
hands trembling, terrified this is it, a heart attack. But it's not
your heart. It's withdrawal.

And I know what else is racing through your head: fear.
Not just about your body, but about what comes next. What
does life even look like without drinking? How will you survive
work dinners, celebrations, stressful days, social awkwardness,
or even boredom without it? You have spent years believing
drinking was just part of your job, part of who you are. Now,
all of that is cracking apart.

I'm you, eight years down the road. eight years sober. And I want to tell you something straight. It's going to be hard, but it will be worth it in ways you can't see right now.

There are going to be moments, especially early on, when it takes everything just to stay sober for one more hour. There will be parties where you feel like a ghost because you are not drinking while everyone else does. There will be celebrations that feel a little empty at first. There will be nights when feelings show up sharp and raw, because alcohol is not there to blur the edges. But you will also start to notice things, little things, coming back to life.

You will feel stronger than you ever expected. You will develop real skills that help you manage stress and anxiety instead of just numbing them. You will make real connections, deeper than those bar-stool conversations you used to rely on. You will sleep better. You will think clearer. You will show up, really show up, for your family.

And yes, the fear you have about work, about losing your edge if you are not "in the mix" at the bar, that fear is lying to you. In eight years, you will be considered for leadership roles you never thought possible. Not despite being sober, but because of who you have become through sobriety. You will build trust, lead with presence, and relate to people in ways drinking never allowed.

But what matters more than any title is this: you will be a better husband, a better father. You will be present, consistent, and emotionally available. Your son will trust you, and your marriage will deepen in ways your drinking self would not understand. That alone is worth it.

This will not be a straight line. Around Day 43, you will slip, and it will hurt. But it will not define you. That moment will teach you something important. Sobriety is not about perfection. It is about honesty, commitment, and getting back up.

You will lose some things. A few friendships will not survive the change. Some people will not know how to connect without alcohol in the mix. But what you gain is so much more. You get real mornings, quiet pride, the peace of not lying to yourself anymore, and the freedom of no longer spending every day negotiating with a drink.

At some point, not overnight but slowly, you will stop thinking about alcohol all the time. It will not dominate your mind. Sobriety will stop being the main thing about you. It will just be part of who you are, woven into how you live.

What starts tonight on that bathroom floor feels like the end, but it is really a beginning. The beginning of a life that is not perfect, but real. It is full of challenge, yes, but also full of clarity, strength, and genuine joy.

So take it one day at a time. Accept help. Be gentle with yourself. Let go of the fantasy that you have to figure it all out alone. Because you do not. You will have support. You will find community. And little by little, you will build something new.

When you look back years from now, you will not feel shame. You will feel compassion. You will understand that rock bottom was not the end of your story. It was the place you finally found solid ground to build something better.

I am here, eight years down the road. Still growing. Still learning. Still showing up. And I am telling you, the life waiting on the other side of this is better than anything alcohol ever gave you.

You have got this.

With love and respect,

Yourself, Eight Years Sober

Chapter Fourteen

Bonus: The Sober Toolkit That Actually Works

T HANK YOU FOR READING this far. Making it to the end of this book means you're serious about change or at least open to seeing what a different path could look like. I'm grateful you've spent your time with these stories, and I hope some of what you've read here has made your own journey feel a little less lonely.

I know how challenging it can be to face real-life situations where cravings sneak up or old habits call your name. That's exactly why I created the Sober Toolkit, a collection of practical strategies, quick reminders, and real-world tips you can turn to when you need something that works in the moment. These are the same tools I've leaned on myself, and they've helped not just me but many others stay steady and keep moving forward.

If you want an extra boost, some honest encouragement, or just a practical game plan for the next tough event, I'd love for you to check out the toolkit. Use the link or QR code below to visit the website, where you can instantly download it. It's my way of saying thank you for reading, and of sharing something that's helped me and so many others. Whether you're at day one or year five, the toolkit is there for you whenever you need it—and you might be surprised by how much a simple idea or new approach can help right when you need it most.

Thank you.

Author Howard Kane

https://selfcarejourneybooks.com/books/double-life-of-a-high-functioning-alcoholic/

This page intentionally left blank.

www.ingramcontent.com/pod-product-compliance
Lightning Source LLC
Chambersburg PA
CBHW062319120626
46546CB00013B/2098